What Will I Do With My Money?

What Will I Do With My Money?

How Your
Personality
Affects Your
Financial
Behavior

RAY LINDER

NORTHFIELD PUBLISHING
CHICAGO

ISBN: 1-881273-33-4

1 3 5 7 9 10 8 6 4 2

Printed in the United States of America

*To my wife, Christine,
and my girls, Diandra and Cassandra.
The joy I receive
from the richness of your personalities
is priceless.*

Contents

EXERCISES

Acknowledgments

I am truly grateful and humbled by the opportunity to write this, my third book, and I must acknowledge those people that have shared in this project.

I must first thank my mom for giving me my first exposure to personality theory through the Myers-Briggs Type Indicator. True to my personality, though, I debated the results! She had the foresight many years ago to see its implications and the far reaching impact this tool would have.

Moody Press is a joy to work with. I especially tip my hat to acquisitions manager Jim Bell, who somehow finds the energy to deal with me and my stream of consciousness ideas; general editor Jim Vincent, whose great skill and sensitivity I greatly trust; publicist Cessandra Dillon, who's always finding people for me to talk to (as if I'm not always doing that myself); and author relations manager Linda Haskins, who indeed relates well. Moody Press has believed in me and their excitement about the idea for this book got me excited to write it.

The Personality Institute of the Southern Tier (New York City) has been very cooperative and supportive of my personality type work. And they know their stuff, too!

I am thankful for all the people that took surveys, answered questions, shared personal stories, and generally endured my obsession with money and personality.

Finally, I appreciate the encouragement of my friends Chester Rowe and Rich Lewis, who remain friends even though I spend all my time writing rather than beating them at basketball; Valerie Facemire for all of her introverted cyberspace encouragement; and at Cornerstone Chapel, Marilyn Nestor and Tracy Levy (what are we doing for lunch today, ladies?), Pastor Gary Hamrick and the rest of the staff and church family.

INTRODUCTION

A New Approach to Money Management

Forget everything you've learned about money. That's right. Forget it! Most of it's based upon worthless fallacies and myths anyway. But forget about the facts, too. Forget about budgets and tax avoidance strategies and mutual funds and hot stocks. Forget about retirement planning and debt reduction. Forget about all the investment advice: "Diversify to reduce risk"; "Buy term and invest the difference." Toss it.

All this well-intentioned traditional advice doesn't work because it ignores the most important factor in the success of personal financial management—*you and your personality.* You need to set aside what you've learned before and learn something new—how your personality affects your relationship and success with money.

We all have ways of thinking and acting that come natural to us. *Personality* is a consistent pattern of attitudes and actions. All forms of human behavior are a function of how our thinking affects our attitudes and actions. An important part of our personality is how we think and feel about money. Because money is such a pervasive influence in society, this influence cannot be underestimated. The average American spends approximately 50 percent of his or her waking hours thinking about money. Therefore, our thoughts and attitudes about money underlie most of our behaviors.

The overabundance of financial education on wealth-creating strategies is missing the most important point of all: Money must be used in a way that satisfies not just the senses but the soul. We don't really want money. What we really want is emotional and psychological satisfaction that comes when we know and satisfy our inner needs. Our money decisions that take into account those needs are wise decisions. That's what this book is about, recognizing our unique temperament and its needs and how that affects our wants, needs, and desires, and how it should affect our money decisions.

Despite greatly increased personal wealth, the number of people calling themselves "very happy" has steadily declined since 1957. Personal disposable income doubled between 1956 and 1988, yet the percentage of Americans saying they were "pretty well satisfied with [my] present financial situation" dropped from 42 to 30 percent![1]

The great and rising financial prosperity most Americans enjoy is clear evidence of our skill in accumulating money. So why are people so unsatisfied with their money despite having more of it and more advice on how to manage it? Because much of what we've learned about money comes from misinformation that unintentionally leads us astray three ways:

- The advice is true, but like a fortune cookie, is too broad to be relevant.
- The advice perpetuates fallacies that prevent us from thinking deeper by providing simple, and often contradictory, answers to complex problems. We hear "money is evil," "greed is good"; "smart people are rich," and "anybody can be rich"; we're told "rich people are happy" and later "rich people are unhappy."
- It leads us to believe that financial freedom is just a matter of simple arithmetic: raise income, cut expenses, invest the difference, track everything with a budget, and life will be great!

What is needed instead is a model of self-understanding that allows us to discern what money really means to us and what ways of earning and spending it will give us the most satisfaction. Such satisfaction will be deeper than simple happiness, which comes and goes with circumstances—usually how much money we have. The result of such satisfaction will be a true

contentment that comes from using money in a personally fulfilling manner. This satisfaction is found on three key as-
sumptions:

1. understanding that money is not an end unto itself, but
   a tool that serves as a means to ends;
2. understanding that the only ends that matter are psychological, emotional, and spiritual rather than material; and
3. believing that it is desirable and possible to know what
   these ends are.

When you understand who you are in relation to money,
you will gain insight into the attitudes you have towards money, why you have those attitudes, and how your attitudes affect
your financial success or failure. You will change your financial
behavior in ways that are personally meaningful, instead of im-
plementing some financial wealth-creating strategy.

Do this and you will master your money. You will make investments that will increase your self-worth as well as your
net worth. You will work hard even though it seems that you're
hardly working. Equally important, you will get off the mon-
ey-spending treadmill that takes you nowhere but still wears
you out.

The word *wealth* at one time referred to a holistic sense of
overall well-being, but over time its meaning has concerned
itself only with financial matters. Benjamin Franklin said that,
"The more a man has, the more he wants. Instead of its filling
a vacuum, it makes one." If money doesn't buy happiness it's
because we don't truly understand what makes us happy.
Whether we feel rich or poor, a slave to money or freed by it,
making ends meet or meeting our ends, has little to do with how
much money we have but whether we feel satisfied when we
earn and spend it. We must recapture how to be wealthy without money.

Satisfaction with money first comes from using it in ways
that are most meaningful to individuals. *If you are going to be
able to manage your money with success, you must have an awareness and understanding of your money personality.* Your financial

house can be put into order much easier if it is built upon a solid foundation of self-awareness. When you become successful in answering the question, "What will I do with my money?" you will become more skillful in using money as the tool it was intended to be—a paper asset that you can exchange for personally meaningful emotional and psychological benefits.

It is possible to eliminate much of the stress and confusion that comes from using money in unproductive ways when you conform your financial behavior to your unique money personality.

The purpose of this book is to guide you through a journey of self-discovery that will help you attain all that wealth was intended to be. Part 1, "The Meaning of Money," begins the self-discovery process with an introspective look at your money attitudes, where they came from, and whether you think your relationship with money is a good one or a bad one.

Part 2, "Your Personality and Money," introduces the fascinating notion that it is actually your innate personality that is the primary contributor to both financial success and satisfaction. What you think is what you do and what you think is a function of who were you born to be. At birth, you were given a personality with predictable behavior dispositions that were designed to fill the needs and values of your personality. As a result you developed a specific form of intelligence that determines what uses of money you will tend to enjoy most.

Self-awareness is only meaningful if it used to make positive changes. Part 3, "Mind Over Money," shows you how to use what you've learned about yourself to finally accomplish what you've always wanted: satisfaction with money regardless of the amount you have.

The goal of this book is to help you see money not as an end to itself but as a tool that enhances your life personally and interpersonally. *What Will I Do with My Money?* can reduce the stress and confusion surrounding money by helping you master the most important factor of all—you!

PART ONE

The Meaning of Money

CHAPTER ONE

The Value
of Money

"A penny for your thoughts."

—John Heywood

M oney. People can't seem to talk about it or even think about it without becoming emotional. Whether that emotion is rapture, rage, excitement, enthusiasm, fear, frustration, denial, or depression, almost everybody feels something about money. Just as the intense pain of a migraine headache makes it difficult to see, our intense feelings about money make it difficult to get a clear sense of what it does to our lives.

Money is one of the most powerful motivators of human behavior. It makes some people run to it. It makes some people run from it. But few people can be still around it.

Money tells us how we behave. Think of these expressions that sometimes describe people's adult lives: We keep up with the Joneses, climb the corporate ladder, pinch pennies, shop 'til we drop. We're born with a silver spoon in our mouth, have a Midas touch, own geese that lay golden eggs and cars that nickel-and-dime us. And for much of our working lives we chase pots of gold at the end of rainbows.

At times, money even defines us. Some of us are "thrifty" or "spendthrift"; "frugal Fannies" or "shopaholics"; "haves" or "have–nots"; "low-rent" or "high roller." In terms of those who do marketing demographics, we are "lower class," "middle class," or "upper class." It's as if we are some biological species based upon financial condition. In fact, one of the most frequently asked questions to someone we've just met is, "What do you do for living?"

AN ECONOMIC TOOL AND MUCH, MUCH MORE

Money, as defined by Webster's dictionary, is an economic tool, a "medium of exchange." Thus, we trade our physical labor for paper money and then exchange our paper money (or credit!) for the material goods we want. But money is much more than simply an economic tool. It is also psychological currency that buys emotional satisfaction. Money touches the essence of who we are and stirs our souls in ways that few things can.

In fact, there's a sense in which money talks to part of our society—always by saying goodbye. First, it says goodbye to the typical family who struggles to work more hours yet still spends more money than they've earned; or to family members who vainly squandered hundreds, even thousands of dollars each year on gambling and lottery tickets.

Second, money says goodbye to the married: Conflicts over money are a leading cause of divorce. Money produces deep conflicts between husbands and wives as it exposes differences in personality, lifestyles, beliefs, and goals. These tensions pull on a marriage because money often reveals our most closely held values, and when those values are violated, many of us react forcefully.

Third, money says goodbye to the living: It is the leading cause of murder and a major contributor of depression and suicide. "Money stress blamed in 3 deaths" read the headline of an article whose graphic nature was exceeded only by its familiarity. "The outburst of gunfire in Reston [Va.] that left three people dead was the result of 'financial stress' in the family," the news account began. "Police would not say what kind of difficulties led 40-year old [Joe Smith] to shoot and kill his 36-year old wife, and 7-year-old son, and wound his 11-year-old daughter, then take his own life."[1]

Money not only talks loudly, it can blur our vision. It's been said that money blinds us to everything not related to ourselves. A priest was speaking to a wealthy businessman who the priest suspected had too strong an attachment to money. The priest asked the man to look out a window and to tell him what he saw. The businessman described the beautiful blue sky, a lush green field, and birds flying between the trees.

Then the priest held up a mirror and once again asked the businessman what he saw.

"Myself, of course."

"Now, what's the difference between the two pieces of glass?" the priest asked.

"Well, one has been painted on a side so it can reflect only the person looking at it."

The businessman paused and realized the priest's point. The one piece of glass had been covered with a coat of silver paint that prevented seeing what was there and allowed the man only to see himself. Money is like a mirror in that it permits us only to see ourselves while it obscures the reality of other life around us.[2]

DOES MONEY BUY HAPPINESS?

America is far and away the world's greatest economic power. The average American's annual income is ten times his middle-class counterpart overseas. Yet, as noted in the introduction, despite rising financial prosperity most Americans feel little financial satisfaction. Does money buy happiness? Clearly it does not. Money has not and cannot meet our deepest psychological needs.

Part of the dissatisfaction that many adults feel is due to poor to fair money management, despite explosive growth in stockbrokers, financial planners, estate planners, and insurance salespeople; not to mention self-help books, magazines and newsletters, more seminars and workshops. With all that information, we still have to account for:

- A record bankruptcy rate during a time of unparalleled economic prosperity;
- Americans spending outpacing their income resulting in a negative national savings rate;
- Four of every five marriages experiencing financial conflict.

Clearly some form of restraint is necessary. But even with better money management, our biggest money problem will remain. That's because almost all wealth-creating strategies leave out the most important point of all: *We must use money in a way that satisfies not just the senses but the soul.*

On the surface, the mechanics of money seem simple enough: work and earn money; want and spend money. But underlying this mathematical simplicity of earn, spend, and save, your income is an emotional complexity that makes money very confusing. Money simply bewilders us. Because we don't know where we *are* with it, we don't know where to *go* with it. Despite all the intensity we have about money, we really don't know how we feel about it. How else do you account for these paradoxes:

- 74 percent of Americans think our society is too materialistic, yet 78 percent say that having a house, car or other nice things is very or fairly important;
- 71 percent think that greed is a sin against God, yet 84 percent would like to have more money;[3]
- fewer Americans are "very happy" today than in the 1950s despite earning and buying twice as much as they did then[4]—yet when asked what hampers the search for the "good life," most responded, "more money"?[5]

The truth is that money mystifies us. We just don't know what we really believe about money. We can't live with it, yet we can't live without it. We want more of it even though spending more of it won't make us any happier. The typical American spends 50 percent of his waking hours thinking about money, yet all that this financial daydreaming has produced is, in the main, a cultural nightmare.

YOUR MONEY ATTITUDE

About Attitude

Part of your money personality is your attitudes toward money. An attitude is how we feel emotionally about something. Since it's clear that we all have emotions regarding money, it follows that each of us has a money attitude. How does that affect you? If your money attitude is positive and healthy, then you will tend to exchange your money for experiences that foster financial growth and personal satisfaction. If, on the other hand, your money attitude is negative and harmful, then your money will be like a mist, dissipating itself with little noticeable impact other than the emptiness and frustration it leaves behind.

Before you can manage money successfully, you need to understand what your money attitude is, why it is, and how it developed. This insight will help your money attitude become your greatest financial asset. What is needed is a model of self-understanding that allows us to discern what money really means to us and what ways of earning and spending it will give us the most satisfaction. Such satisfaction will be deeper than simple happiness, which comes and goes with circumstances—usually how much money we have. It will reflect a true joy and contentment that comes from using money in a personally fulfilling manner. That is what wealth was meant to be.

Most of us fail to realize the degree to which our money attitude affects our financial habits and more importantly, the amount of satisfaction we get from our money. While we tend to think that our financial behavior is related to how much money we have, the fact is that there is a much stronger connection between our often unconscious, unknown feelings about money and the way we spend, give, borrow, and invest it.

Learning Your Money Attitude

Although money is supposedly just an economic tool intended to be exchanged for other things, for such small pieces of paper and metal it sure carries a lot of weight. What does money mean to you? How do you feel about it? In spite of the strong relationship between what we think and how we act, most of us have not given serious thought to what we think about money.

How we see money is a statement of how we see ourselves. The first step to determining what to do with your money is to develop an awareness of how you feel emotionally about money and your relationship with it. A profitable exercise to begin understanding your money attitude is to establish a financial baseline, according to Olivia Mellan, author and consultant in the field of money-conflict resolution.[6] Mellan suggests that you articulate your own personal feelings about money by coming up with two lists, one positive and the other negative. Complete exercise 1, which is adapted from Mellan's work.

Exercise 1

YOUR MONEY ATTITUDE: A FINANCIAL BASELINE

On a sheet of paper, prepare two lists. On the first list, show all areas of your personal finances that give you pride or pleasure. You should have at least two, but it could be many more. For example, your positive list might include responses such as:

1. I have a budget and stick to it.
2. I have clean credit.
3. I'm a generous giver.
4. I have over $100,000 in my retirement plan.

Next, describe two or more aspects or attitudes about your personal finances that you're not comfortable with, maybe even embarrassed or guilty about. These might be things such as:

1. I have too much debt.
2. I am overextended financially.
3. I have no savings or investments.
4. I have trouble giving money or spending money on other people.

Which list is longer for you or the easier to come up with, the positive list or the negative one? How has each list affected your life, including significant relationships? Have the positive entries caused any stresses that you may have unconsciously omitted from your negative list? For example, is the fact that you don't have a problem with spending too much money because you have a problem of spending too much time at work? Now is the time to bring these emotions out into the light.

SOURCE: Adapted from Olivia Mellan, *Money Harmony* (New York: Walker and Company, 1994), 17.

As you consider both lists and determine your financial baseline, realize that each list has value. The negative list is your catalyst to change the things you don't like about your money attitude. When you finally get sick and tired of being sick and tired, you'll no longer be willing to tolerate your negative emotions and you'll be motivated to change.

Changes in firmly entrenched habits don't come easily. It's sometimes easier to live down to our own low expectations than to move emotionally into new territory. That's why the positive list is so important. While the negative list is your catalyst to change, the positive list provides your confidence to change.

Now that you have a baseline—a general assessment of your money attitude—it's time to consider what's behind our feelings about money. But to do that we'll need to make a brief digression to the field of economics.

HOW WE USE UTILES

Economists, those who study and analyze the production, distribution, and consumption of goods and services, have a fancy word for an important concept: *utiles.* Utiles are a theoretical measure of satisfaction, a way of quantifying how useful things or activities are to us. Just as the atom is the basic building block of all physical matter, the utile is the essential element of all economic matters.

When we unconsciously assign values to things and activities, we give them a number of utiles. If something is very satisfying to us, it can be said that it provides us with a lot of utiles. On the other hand, things not very useful to us give us few utiles.

The reason utiles are so important is that they make us decide how we use our money. In a sense, utiles define us as they motivate us to self-expression through our use of money.

For example, my wife can attest that she's never described me by using the words "handy" and "man" in the same sentence. Therefore, a trip to Home Depot will generate very few utiles for me—except for those created by accomplishing a task on my "Honey-Do" list!

But a trip to Tower Records? Now that's a different story altogether! As I walk down the aisles of compact discs, I feel utiles

I didn't know I had trying to express themselves. I get the same way in large bookstores. CD's and books are very useful to me because music and reading give me great personal satisfaction. Therefore, I express that satisfaction economically by spending money on them.

My wife loves quilting and crafts. Her utiles come from fabric—fabric on bolts, fabric in catalogs, fabric in every color, texture, weight, and price imaginable. She can feel her utiles rising each time she goes into her favorite fabric store. Fabric and other crafting materials are useful to Christine because they give her a great deal of satisfaction. These are the activities that she enjoys spending money on.

Whether it's for computers, sports, clothes, tools, cars, or stuffed animals, all of us have utiles. We have a large number of utiles for the things we care deeply about and very few for things that don't matter much. While it is true that theoretical abstractions such as "large number of utiles" or "few utiles" cannot truly be measured, the concept is helpful in that it defines an internal, unconscious force that drives our financial decisions. Utiles help us to better understand how we use—or abuse—our relationship with money. This concept will be even more helpful if we understand where our utiles are and where they come from, which is the point of the next two exercises.

LIFE PRIORITIES AND MOTIVATIONS

Five Key Domains

Many psychologists and sociologists classify our lives as having five domains. We draw energy and enthusiasm for life from these domains. The five domains are: (1) physical, relating to the body, material things, or our physical surroundings; (2) mental, relating to the mind and intellect; (3) emotional, relating to subjective feelings or sensibilities in regards to yourself or important interpersonal relationships; (4) social, relating to family, friendly relations or companionship, or occupied with matters affecting human welfare, including business; and (5) spiritual, relating to the immaterial, supernatural, and/or sacred aspects of life.

24

These five domains form a major component of our money personalities, because we will tend to try to organize our lives around the domains that produce the greatest sense of personal satisfaction. In other words, we have different amounts of utiles in each of the five domains according to their importance to us. Certainly, the desire to seek enjoyment in each domain is a built-in part of our being. But the ongoing interest in the spiritual domain suggests that our deepest needs are spiritual. Jesus, the founder of the Christian faith, concluded that living to please God should be the focus of every man and woman.[7] He told listeners that the search for pleasure, wealth, and success outside of a relationship with God is not only a vain pursuit, but unnecessary because God knows our needs and is committed to meeting them.

While our deepest needs are spiritual, each of us has utiles in the other domains that define unfulfilled needs. Money is one of the important ways that we try to fulfill those needs. Most uses of money affect several domains. For example, buying a house can be an expression of satisfying a physical need (amount or configuration of living space); a social need (location of schools, distance from friends or family); or an emotional need (security; sense of belonging). Buying a book may gratify us mentally (learning new things); physically (providing relaxation); or socially (discussing the book with others).

However, in most cases our uses of money are dominated by needs coming out of one primary domain. For Lucy, buying a house was mostly a matter of fulfilling a social need. She wanted to be a permanent part of a community. Ed reads mostly to expand his knowledge in the field of Civil War history— satisfying a need from his mental domain.

Finding Your Priorities

Complete exercise 2 to determine those areas (domains) in your life that have the highest priority to you.

Exercise 2

THE PERSONAL IMPORTANCE
OF THE FIVE DOMAINS

Take a moment to rank the first four domains in order of their importance to you:

_____ Physical

_____ Mental

_____ Emotional

_____ Social

The spiritual domain is omitted because of its potential to be so pervasive that it influences desires in all of the other domains. Instead, consider how important a role this part of your life plays in your financial decisions. Be honest as your evaluate the role of the spiritual in your financial decision making. Select which answer applies best to you as you complete this statement: "For me, during financial decision making the spiritual domain plays:

_____ a very important role

_____ a fairly important role

_____ a minor role

_____ no role at all

The purpose of the exercise is to draw your attention to the areas of your life that have the highest priority to you. Where you are energized is an essential ingredient of your money personality. Using money for activities within your favorite domains is key to feeling financially fulfilled. If, however, a lot of your money is being used outside of your life's priorities, you stand a good chance of becoming depressed and unresponsive to the world.

Motivation

Now consider the motivations that underlie your financial behaviors. Motives are emotions or desires that operate on our wills and stimulate us to act. Sometimes the stimuli moving us to action are external, such as inducements, incentives, or coercion. At other times, the stimuli are internal and arise from our personal temperament or disposition.

Unlike biological drives, such as hunger or thirst, there is no physical need met simply by having money. However, there are significant psychological motives that cause us to use money the way that we do. Here are six common motives for financial action: (1) desire for financial gain; (2) avoiding financial loss; (3) comfort and convenience; (4) security and protection; (5) pride of ownership; and (6) emotional satisfaction. Look at these six. What are the top three motives for *your* financial action? Those three probably are driving many of your financial actions.

Motivation is an important, yet often hidden aspect of our money personality. Many of the financial decisions we make are in response to powerful motivating forces that compel us to act in predictable ways. Awareness and acceptance of your financial motivations is crucial to finding satisfaction with money.

Our life priorities and our financial motivations are an extension of our values—a personal determination of things that are important to us, that supply meaning to life, that define who we are and why we do the things we do. In the next section, we will look more closely at the subject of financial values.

WHAT ARE YOUR FINANCIAL VALUES?

Values are the deep-rooted beliefs you have about what is good, desirable, and innately worthwhile. They are related to and arise from your inborn temperament but can be shaped by your experiences in your home, in your faith, and in your community. To value something is to have a pervasive desire for objects, feelings, and/or experiences either for yourself, for others, or both. Awareness of our values helps us understand why certain things mean so much to us.

All your life you have had to and will continue to make choices based upon your values. And your values definitely come into play when you have to decide how to use your money. With our values being so important, identifying them is desirable and necessary in decision making. That's what you should do in exercise 3 that follows. Please complete exercise 3 to clarify your current values.

Exercise 3
CLARIFYING MY VALUES

Which three statements are the most important for you personally? Which three are the least important?	Most Important	Least Important
1. To have people like me	❒	❒
2. To do things for my family and others	❒	❒
3. To be able to do things I want to do	❒	❒
4. To do new and different things often	❒	❒
5. To have friends	❒	❒
6. To contribute to the happiness of my family	❒	❒
7. To do what is right according to my beliefs	❒	❒
8. To have as many of the good things of life as I can	❒	❒
9. To be able to do things well	❒	❒

SOURCE: Adapted from *Management, Analysis and Planning for Families*, Virginia Cooperative Extension Publication 354-023, 1992, 2–9.

Because money is such a crucial factor in everyday life, it is vital that you use it in ways that support your personal values. When your money use does not match your values, stress will definitely be created. The stress is twofold: (1) you are not making good decisions, those that support your values; and (2) the constant lack of validation of what you think is important will eventually damage your self-esteem. You will think less of yourself, which has many negative implications for all of life not just your finances.

Often we don't become aware of our values until we experience direct conflict with people or circumstances over our values. Values are personal, and often conflicts with others are likely if we don't articulate to ourselves and others what our values are. Therefore, you should acknowledge your financial values (which you determined in the previous exercise). This is a necessary step if you are to achieve true wealth.

BEGINNING THE JOURNEY

There is a strong relationship between what we think and how we act. The problem is that most of us have never given any attention to how we think and feel about money. The goal of this chapter has been to help guide you through a process of self-discovery in order to establish where you are psychologically with money.

Ancient sailors navigated the oceans by using the North Star to establish their bearings so they would know how to steer the ship to stay on course. Unlike most other financial self-help materials that futilely presume to navigate you to a pot of gold at the end of the rainbow, this self-discovery could set you on a path of true wealth—a holistic sense of overall well-being— that makes the journey golden rather than the destination. It is a path that is uniquely yours because you are a unique individual with attitudes, priorities, motives, and values—utiles— all your own.

The first leg of your journey has been introspective; the next will be a retrospective examination of your money memories. When you make the connection between what you learned in the past and how you behave in the present, you will be better able to navigate changes in the future.

CHAPTER TWO

Your Money Memories

Our memories are independent of our wills.
It is not easy to forget.

—Richard Sheridan

"My parents never taught me about money" is a commonly expressed explanation for people's financial dilemmas. The fact is that all of us were taught by the financial behaviors modeled for us by our parents. The first things most of us learned was that you rarely talk about money, but when you do, you "talk" about it very emotionally. Of course, our parents were taught by their parents the same way. Therefore, most people suffer from the same disadvantage: generations of noncommunication, miscommunication, and poor communication about money.

How much of your financial attitudes and behaviors reflect patterns of thought and action modeled to you by your parents? The purpose of this chapter is to have you explore your money memories, the learned financial behaviors from your family history. What we learned directly or indirectly about money in our childhood is a powerful influence on how we'll behave financially as adults.

Separating ourselves from family financial influences can be very difficult. When we become aware of how enmeshed we are with those past influences, we can eventually learn to detach ourselves from them. And that's crucial to the successful mastery of one's money personality. You will be able to relate to money in a way that is consistent with your uniquely held priorities, motives, and values.

That's a critical skill in marriage when each partner brings a separate set of baggage into the couple's emotional cargo space, which has room only for one set of luggage. The money attitudes that you brought to a relationship from the past are quite often the source of money conflicts in the present. What we saw our family doing with money typically becomes our way of managing money. We think that anything that deviates from that way is abnormal, weird, crazy, or dangerous to our financial stability.

FAMILY FINANCIAL HABITS

Let's define a habit. A habit is a routine behavior that is done unconsciously. Habits are learned and refined through frequent repetition. There is nothing intrinsically good or bad about habits. As complex as money seems to be at times, managing money still comes down to four basic habits of spending, giving, saving, and borrowing. Each day your money will be subjected to at least one of these habits, usually with no thought on your part.

While your parents may not have explicitly taught you about financial habits in those four areas, you still learned about them from watching their financial habits. What you observed is bound to have a large influence on how you feel about using your own money in these ways. As playwright Richard Sheridan wrote, "It is not easy to forget." To see how your memories remain and influence your attitude, complete exercise 4 below.

Exercise 4

FAMILY HABITS IN SPENDING, SAVING, GIVING, AND BORROWING

Take out a sheet of paper (or copy this sheet) and answer the questions in each category. You can circle the appropriate option or give a short answer. Then put a put a checkmark (✔) in front of the habit you either practice or agree with.

Spending
1. Did your family operate on a strict budget or just spend freely?
2. Was it important to buy on sale?
3. Which was most important: convenience, quality, or price?

4. What kinds of family vacations did you go on?

5. Did you buy new cars or used and how often did you replace a car?

Saving

1. Did your parents ever discuss any kinds of savings or investment accounts?

2. What was the family's philosophy: "A penny saved is a penny earned," "Save for a rainy day," or "You can't take it with you"?

3. Were you encouraged at an early age to save your own money earned from allowance, gifts, or jobs?

4. Did your parents save for large future expenses like cars, house, college, or retirement?

5. How did your parents save—bank, savings bonds, stocks, mutual funds? This might be an indication of how open to financial risk they were, which would say much about their need for security and perhaps influence your own confidence in money.

Giving

1. Did your parents give to their church or other charitable organizations?

2. Did they give a set amount or percentage of their income?

3. Were your parents generous people in general, sharing time, helping others and volunteering, and encouraging you to do the same?

4. Were there any explicitly communicated values about giving of time, talent, or money?

5. Did your parents give to support social or political causes?

Borrowing

1. Did your family use credit sparingly or freely? Did you see family members frequently charging purchases?

2. Did your parents have any rules against debt, like "never a borrower or lender be" or "owe no man any thing, but to love one another"?

3. Did they pay cash or borrow for large purchases like furniture and appliances?

4. Did a parent ever co-sign a loan for you?

5. Do you recall stress over bills? Were bills paid late? Was there ever a bankruptcy in your family?

Recall from chapter 1 that your money attitude is how you feel emotionally about money. Overall, did your family have a good or bad attitude about their financial habits? Did their attitudes have a positive or negative affect on you and your own financial habits? Are you experiencing stress due to conflicting habits between your parents and your own?

An honest self-assessment in this area of your past will uncover much useful information about your past that is influencing your financial habits today, both positively and negatively.

FAMILY FINANCES: COMMUNICATION, CIRCUMSTANCES, AND BIRTH ORDER

Because we typically don't struggle personally with money until we are adults, we don't connect our present financial stresses with experiences from our past. The reality is that our financial attitudes were shaped by the behaviors modeled to us by our parents as they went through their adult money struggles. Exercise 4 should make clear the role of your parents' financial habits on who you are. Too often, as children seeing the results and emotions of our parents' financial decisions without being part of the process, what we took away was that money was powerful and that money was important. Now, as adults, we have our own unintended perspectives regarding money from the psychological imprints of those observations.

For instance, during one seminar I led where we were exploring money memories, Sheila told the group how money conflicts in her marriage came from the free-spending influence of her mother. Lack of money was not an issue in her family. Her mother spent money as she saw fit and her father did not restrain that behavior. Sheila had a quite a shock when her husband, whose family financial background was much different, tried to put controls on her spending, an unthinkable action given that this was something she never saw her father do. When she realized that her parents' money attitudes were actually harmful in her present financial and relational situation, she learned to detach herself from these attitudes to her ongoing benefit.

During your childhood, your parents affected your money

values in three significant areas: communication, difficult circumstances, and your birth order in the family.

Communication

When it comes to communication and family finances, two cliché statements still apply: "Actions speak louder than words," and "Money talks." What we heard when our family members talked about money was also a part of our financial education (so was how they responded to difficult financial times).

If what our parents did were our primary finance teachers, their thoughts, expressions, and emotions were their teacher's aides. What do you recall about the way your family communicated about money?

1. Did your parents have a philosophy of working together or independently? Was there one person who clearly seemed in charge of the family finances?
2. Were finances for your parents a source of frequent arguments? Were there noticeable differences in their attitudes toward money?
3. When were conflicts dealt with? Immediately, later, or swept under the carpet? How did the parties respond to conflict? Through escalation or withdrawal?

Circumstances

At some time, almost every family faces tough financial issues. How you saw your parents and other family members adapt to difficult financial circumstances probably had a strong impact on you. Even if your financial circumstances don't match those from your family history, implicit in your family's handling of situations were their financial priorities, motives, and values.

For example, Vanessa's father had a business failure when she was eleven years old. He controlled the family finances in a highly independent style. Like many men, he was adept at compartmentalizing his life, and was able to separate the business financial problems from family issues, including the family's finances. What was implied was that money was one thing, the rest of life was another. However, today as a single mom, Vanessa's lack of experience and complete detachment from money has made it difficult for her to feel confident about handling day-to-day family financial issues and connecting those issues to the rest of her life in general.

As you recall your family history, try to determine if any past circumstantial events have shaped your financial behaviors. Here are five key questions to help you recall potential financial challenges growing up: (1) Were there particular circumstances or events in your family that had an effect on its relationship to money? (2) How many children were in your family? What do you recall about how your family dealt with money because of the family's size? (3) Was a wage earner in your family ever out of work? Did a family business fail and was a bankruptcy filed because of the failure? (4) Did a divorce, separation, or death in the family affect its financial condition? (5) Were there any other catastrophic events that contributed to family financial stress?

Birth Order

Are you surprised the subject of birth order appears in a book on money? You shouldn't be; some experts see the child's birth order in the family as an important dynamic in the development of the child's money attitudes.[1] When it came to the financial behaviors modeled to you, you and your siblings may have had "different parents," depending on where each of you were in the order of birth. Some of these dynamics were a product of growing in the experience of rearing children; some were due to different financial stresses caused by additional children.

If you are a first child, and especially the first grandchild, you may have been showered with gifts and special attention; conversely, you may have received fewer financial privileges than later siblings because you were the "lab rat"; that is, you blazed the trail, teaching your parents what "works."

If you are an only child, you probably didn't learn as much about sharing as other children. If you didn't have to share much as a child, you may have difficulty sharing and sacrificing as an adult. Since you had no one to compete with for the family's financial resources, you may have a tendency to expect to continue being treated the same way.

If you are a second, or other middle child, not only was money perhaps a scarcer resource, but so was time. Your parents had many demands while caring for multiple children; this may have forced you into developing personal skills faster than your younger siblings had to. This pressure to perform may have been carried over into adulthood, and with it a sense of continually being overwhelmed and not feeling able to satisfy the demands of others. Depending on how you reacted during those formative years, you may find yourself drowning in the continual realities of financial management.

Are you the "baby" in the family? Often the youngest gets used to getting his way. Parents tend to indulge the youngest child. Also, as the demands of the family structure grew, there may have been less time to be involved in the affairs of the youngest child. In some cases, the family financial security improved as career paths moved upward over time, making available more material benefits for you as the youngest than were available to your older siblings.[2]

Think about the influence that your family structure may have had on you in terms of your attitudes toward money. Have you talked to your parents or siblings about the family history in terms of life around the time of the birth of each child? If not, you may want to learn about any changes that were made in anticipation of, or because of, additions to the family. Was there a new house? A bigger used car? Why and how frequently were their job moves or career changes? Did Mom leave or enter the workforce as a result of a new family member?

In addition, as an adult, have you ever discussed or compared your growing up experiences with your spouse or close friends?

Answering the above questions can help you to recognize and deal with some of the attitudes you may have toward money management as well as toward another family member. This type of exploration may lead you to a treasure trove that contains healing of long-term unresolved issues, valuable insight into your own money attitudes, and practical advice on how to manage difficult, real world money problems.

FAMILY TRADITIONS REGARDING
WORK, RELIGIOUS TRAINING, AND MONEY

Work and Money

Almost every family has its own traditions regarding money and work. Again, implied in these traditions are preconceived beliefs and attitudes about the meaning and importance of money. Quite often, tradition, practices, and money values become so intertwined that the value of individual people gets lost.

We all probably know of someone whose career choice was determined early on—probably at birth!—by their parents. John was to be a doctor because his father was a doctor and his grandfather a doctor, and his great-grandfather a doctor and so on. All of us probably know of someone who was trained as early as possible to take a role in the family business. As we'll see later in part 2, which deals with innate personality preferences, these unilateral career choices aren't always positive if people are not predisposed to have talent and interest in the fields selected for them.

To recognize your own family traditions regarding money and work, answer these questions:

1. Was there pressure to choose a particular career path? Why—for reasons of money or reasons of tradition or both?
2. Were women encouraged or discouraged from seeking careers? Did your mother ever work outside the home? If so, was it because she wanted to or because she had to for financial reasons?
3. Was more work associated with earning more money? Did your father advocate long working hours?
4. Was your childhood allowance connected with specific tasks? Did you have to work after-school and summer jobs? Did you have to work while in college?

Religious Training

Religious beliefs can have such a pervasive influence on our financial behaviors that they have the potential to supersede all of our other attitudes.

38

Many people don't realize it, but the subject of money and possessions is one of the dominant themes of Christian teaching. Its lessons illustrate the core principle that God has entrusted money to us for His purposes. Therefore, we should use it in a way that balances practical, relational, and eternal perspectives.

Some families are unaware of these faith lessons. Others prefer to keep matters of faith separate from matters of finance, although such an attitude is branded unwise by the Scriptures. Still others are so dogmatic in their beliefs that they are very intolerant of other religious views about money. Any of these family attitudes toward money can create ambivalence or hostility toward the influence of religion on one's financial practices.

In Lauren's case, her parents believed that money was "the root of all evil."[3] In spite of impressive academic and professional credentials, Lauren has tended to work in relatively low-paying jobs, affirming her parents' belief that if there is anything she needs, "the Lord will provide." She admits to viewing offers for significantly higher paying work with suspicion that they may tempt her to become too "worldly."

Here are four key questions to help you determine the role of your religious training on your attitudes toward money.

1. What religious principles did your family apply in the management of the family finances?
2. Was money considered "the root of all evil"?
3. Was money considered a sign of blessing?
4. During times of financial stress, how much did religious practices influence how the family handled the situation? Did they willingly or begrudgingly accept benevolent help from others, or refuse taking "a handout"?

Are You Rebelling Against Your Family Money Influences?

To the extent that our parents' habits and attitudes caused us feelings of guilt, shame, fear, rejection, or inadequacy, we will reject those habits and attitudes to prevent further emotional pain. Using something external like money to resolve internal issues is a complicated issue, and a successful outcome is not very likely. The results often end up continuing to hurt us, just in different ways. One typical outcome is an irrational belief in financial fallacies, the topic of the next chapter.

Another more dangerous result of unresolved anger against our parents is carrying that unresolved anger into another personal relationship. Growing up without concrete expressions of love from her parents and with a family that went without many of the material things her peers had, Aubrey dreamed of a husband who would generously provide for her financial needs. Although she finally found such a man, it didn't take long to realize that they had both a poor marriage and poor financial situation. Despite their profligate spending habits, her husband's frustrated lament was, "There's never enough for her. I just can't ever seem to make her happy." For her part, Aubrey found her feelings of love for her husband waning over time.

Aubrey wasn't happy because extravagantly spending money wasn't what she really wanted. No matter how much she bought, the good feelings were short-lived—and so she spent even more, which only made her marriage and money worse off. Her husband, of course, proved an inadequate replacement for what was missing from Aubrey's life. It was never really the money that she was after but the assurance and security of her parents' affection that was missing from her childhood.

THE INFLUENCE OF
PEERS, CULTURE, AND SOCIETY

Our Peers

While family experts and researchers debate the degree, no one can deny that friends and peers play a dominant role in our lives. If the first five years or so of our lives were influenced by family relationships, the nearly 14,000 hours we spent in school during the subsequent twelve years will clearly make our peer group another major life influence. Consciously or unconsciously, our self-image today has been influenced somewhat by comparisons to actual or desired peer groups. Therefore, we will try to achieve the economic status and emulate the financial behaviors of these peer groups. This can cause great anxiety if a particular peer group is very different financially than our family's or if we find it difficult to actually attain the lifestyle of our desired group.

Answer these five questions to better understand the role of your childhood and early adult peers in shaping your current attitudes toward money:

1. Were any of your peers' families more affluent than yours, and did this influence your attitude toward money? Did you see yourself as living on the "other side of the tracks" or "on the right side of town"?

2. Did you choose your friends based upon their lifestyle? Did your friends choose you because of yours?

3. Did you find yourself wishing for certain things that you hoped would impress others?

4. What were your emotions in regards to your peer group: shame, envy, hurt, security, love, pride?

5. Were there any emotionally memorable incidents from your past that involved your peers and your relationship to them economically? Are these incidents motivating any of your financial behaviors today?

Our Culture

The economic characteristics of some generations have been profound enough to create distinct financial cultures. These cultures tend to have easily identifiable and commonly held financial outlooks and attitudes about money. These outlooks and attitudes range from the very fiscally conservative and sometimes fearful economic outlook of Depression-era children to the optimism and aggressive financial practices of the baby boomers and baby busters and to the financial apathy of generation X and post-generation X.

In addition to influencing each generation's economic characteristic, the prevailing culture will influence money attitudes regarding male and female roles and racial relationships. Expected roles of men and women in dealing with money affect single as well as married adults; similarly culture influences our attitudes toward different races. Whether you are African-American, Asian,

Caucasian, or Latino has serious implications for your money personality.

As a minority, I have my own sensitivity to cultural issues as they relate to race and money. As a young boy traveling with my family, I remember my parent's frustrations at trying to find a motel that had rooms available for a black family. Much later in my life, I listened to my dad comment at his retirement as a vice-president at a major utility company how he grew up near a utility company in the inner city. As a young boy, he believed that he would never be able to work at such a place because of his race.

How my parents dealt with such situations shaped my financial values and behaviors as they intentionally sought to teach their children to overcome the cultural biases against us. We were also freely exposed to inner-city life and the economic consequences of not overcoming the culture's bias. There is no question that these memories continue to be a major part of my money personality.

If you are a minority, you may have fear or misconceptions about what you can or cannot do with money and jobs. If you are white, you may have comparatively higher expectations set by your parents; these can either help or hinder you in such areas as career and spending plans.

Of course, stereotypes about the roles of men and women regarding money continue to influence single and married adults. For men, these stereotypes would include that they know how to "do money," to be the primary wage earner of the family, to be competitive and independent. The simple translation of these stereotypes is that the more money you have, the more of a man you are.

For women, the cultural stereotypes are quite different. Although they are definitely changing, the stereotypes for women concerning money are generally negative. For the most part women are expected to not be able to do money ("that's a male thing"), to be unable to make tough financial decisions, and to be more concerned about family concerns than making money. The simple and sad translation of these stereotypes is that femininity and finance don't mix.

Whether racial or gender related, the culture probably has given you money memories—both positive and negative. Keep in mind that your financial attitude and outlook have been affected by: (1) your generation's economic character; (2) your beliefs about race; and (3) the degree to which you fit or don't fit the culture's expectations about men, women, and money.

Our Society

A final key influence of our money memories is the affect of the society in which we live. In America, we live in an instant-gratification society where you can get your dinner in five minutes either from the microwave or the drive-through window. Television has given us a world where we can solve all kinds of problems in thirty minutes, or about half that if you take out all the appeals to get you to use your credit card. We have become used to an existence where we can fulfill our "needs" as fast as we feel them.

In addition, sociological studies show that the buying patterns of those around us determine what we buy. What we want is what our neighbors and coworkers have even if we can't afford it. Even when families have the misfortune of seeing their income drop, economists have discovered a tendency called the "Jones-effect"—from the expression "keeping up with the Joneses"—where people force themselves to keep up with others even when their ability to do so no longer exists.

And credit cards allow us to artificially spend for possessions even when we don't have the money available for them. Furthermore, society pressures our money attitudes in one other way. Through the media of television and movies we view a common lifestyle—typically higher middle class and sometimes upper class—that we can aspire to. The clothes, the cars, the homes, and the fancy restaurants of most TV and movie characters look appealing. Generally, those lifestyles are beyond the level that most of us can afford. But with easily acquired credit—another characteristic of modern America—we can emulate almost anyone we want to compare ourselves to.

MAXIMIZING THE MERIT
OF OUR MONEY MEMORIES

Whether it's the messages from your parents, peers, culture, or society, we can easily feel unfulfilled financially. If you find yourself continually fighting feelings of emptiness and frustration, it may be due to unresolved feelings about your money memories. The influence of our family or those outside can keep us from a satisfying relationship with money. If that's the case, we may need an assertive and objective reevaluation of the messages communicated to us about money to determine if they are, in fact, appropriate for us.

The negative aspects of our money memories now can sustain unhealthy money attitudes—or they can become the catalyst to personal change. Meanwhile, recalling positive memories can give us the confidence to change. The reason for recognizing our family financial past is to objectively determine which of our memories are worth retaining and building on and which need to be discarded as harmful or nonproductive.

We conclude our chapter with a final exercise about your *positive* financial memories. As you answer these questions, recognize that your positive memories can give you the confidence—and the model—for good money habits.

Making the most of our money memories is a critical stop in the journey to true financial satisfaction.

Exercise 5

POSITIVE MONEY MEMORIES

Answer each of the following questions on a separate piece of paper. Then use these positive memories as a model for good money habits.

1. Who in your past modeled positive financial attitudes and behaviors: parents, other relatives, a boss or mentor, someone you learned or read about?
2. What were the most prominent events from your past that molded your money attitudes in a positive manner?
3. What specific financial habits came out of the positive experiences and attitudes modeled to you?
4. Are there specific financial habits that you have not incorporated from any positive past money memories? Why not and what would it take to do so?

CHAPTER THREE

Financial Fallacies

A poor person who is unhappy is in a better position than a rich person who is unhappy. Because the poor person has hope. He thinks money would help.

—*Jean Kerr*

To deceive someone by misleading or causing them to believe something that is not true sounds a lot like telling a lie. Sure enough, the American Heritage Dictionary of the English Language (3rd edition) defines the word *lie* as "to present false information with the intention of deceiving" or "to convey a false image or impression."

Yes, money talks. When it's not saying goodbye—that seems a common occurrence—it usually is telling lies, insidious harmful lies that lead us into ruinous and destructive traps. These lies are financial fallacies, dangerous, yet deeply held, inaccurate beliefs that may underlie our financial attitudes and behaviors. They are dangerous because there is just enough plausibility in them to be believed and enough people believe in them to give them credibility.

These financial fallacies actually come from our society or even from our birth family and peers. Significantly, these fallacies prevent us from thinking deeply about our relationship with money by providing simple, and often contradictory, answers to complex problems: "money is evil," "greed is good"; "smart people are rich," "anybody can be rich"; "rich people are happy," "rich people are unhappy"; and so on.

Just as insidious as the plausibility of financial fallacies is their source. They are often an escape from the pain of unmet emotional needs somewhere in our past, a way that helps us cope with past emotional wounds. Unfortunately, the fallacies also lead us to false expectations about what money should do. Our false beliefs about money may help us cope, but they do not help us heal.

The result is a vain pursuit to get satisfaction from our financial transactions, a pursuit that ends up leaving us as bewildered and helpless as the original emotional pain we were trying to escape from.

WHAT MONEY SEEMS TO SAY

Six fallacies plague the thinking of most Americans, who accept the following lies about money:

1. Achievement. Money says that I do things well.
2. Freedom. Money says that I can have what I want when I want.
3. Respect. Money says that people like me.
4. Power. Money says that I am in charge of my life.
5. Security. Money says that I will always be safe.
6. Happiness. Money says that I enjoy myself.

Money talks, and most people listen to what it says about achievement, freedom, respect, and the rest. Even a lack of money manages to speak loudly. To most Americans, limited funds say: (1) *failure*—"I do things poorly"; (2) *bondage*—"I am imprisoned by my financial state"; (3) *weakness*—"I am not in charge of my life"; (4) *fear*—"I will never be safe and secure"; and (5) *unhappiness*—"I am unhappy because I lack enough money."

The six fallacies are both pervasive and insidious. As we look at each, you may ask yourself whether a family member or yourself has embraced one or more of these.

Financial Fallacy #1: Achievement

The 1980s will remain the decade of high finance, of mergers and megadeals. While the financial press celebrated the exploits of the wheeler-dealers and "masters of the universe," prime-time TV shows such as *Dallas, Dynasty,* and *Falcon Crest* made it clear that money equaled achievement. The decade's heroes were J.R. Ewing and such real-life counterparts like Ivan Boesky and Michael Miliken, all of questionable and even ruthless character. Despite their at-times reprehensible conduct, they were deemed excellent and praiseworthy because of their Midas-like ability to make money.

Many have adopted this standard that having money is achievement because in their past they were not allowed to feel successful. The money-is-achievement fallacy allows them to escape from those wounds by defining their success in terms that are widely accepted and therefore—at least in their minds—irrefutable.

Consider how labels like "upper class" and "lower class" have become so common. Then we developed all of the gradations in between, "middle class," "upper middle class," and "lower middle class." We have created many specific labels for the wealthy, including "affluent," "rich," and "super rich." Then there are the "poor" and those "below poverty level." Our willingness to perpetuate such labels is indicative of how much money matters to us and our sense of accomplishment.

If you take great pride in your financial accomplishments or want to prove your personal worth by increasing your net worth, then be warned! You may be trapped by the fallacy that says with money you do things well.

Financial Fallacy #2: Freedom

One of the most prevalent fallacies of our modern culture is that it is possible to attain financial freedom. Popularized by the financial services and network marketing industries and by get-rich-quick financial gurus, this fallacy suggests that it is a highly desirable goal to accumulate enough money to make whatever choices in life you want. With financial freedom you will no longer have any limitations or restrictions on your life because of money. You can work if you want to, or not work if you want to; you can go wherever you want, do whatever you want, buy whatever you want.

Implicit in the financial freedom fallacy is that if you cannot have whatever you want when you want, it's because you don't have enough money.

The money-is-freedom fallacy is an attempt to escape from the demands of everyday life. When you feel the pressure of bills, bosses, babies, or bad relationships, you become an easy target for this fallacy. In contrast to the money-is-achievement fallacy, the financial freedom fallacy says that the only financial achievement that matters is having enough money that money no longer matters. With enough money you can have independence and choices. In other words, nobody can tell you what you can or cannot do!

You probably have fallen for the fallacy of financial freedom if you feel that with more money you could really have the kind of life you want.

Financial Fallacy #3: Respect

The third fallacy presumes that because we associate our own self-worth with our financial net worth that others do the same. "Money says that people like me," say followers of this fallacy. When we carry this mistaken belief into relationships, whether business or personal, we live under the self-centered notion that our value in life is based upon what we *get* from others rather than what we *do* for others.

Steven Covey, author of *Seven Habits of Highly Effective People,* studied the history of success literature in America and found a disturbing societal shift. Until World War II, a person's ability to earn the respect and admiration of others was based upon how he helped others. Being a hardworking family provider, a caring husband, an attentive father, and a community servant were the characteristics that marked a man worthy of respect.

However, during the 1950s, our values began to change. Soon, having a public image, a positive mental attitude, a craftily written resume, a "connected" network of "gatekeepers", and of course, dressing for success, became more important than character. In other words, we shifted to manipulating others to gain their approval so we can get what we want, rather than manifesting our true selves to gain others' respect by giving them what they need.

Equating money with respect is an attempt to escape the pain of not feeling connected to others. It is using money to provide a boost to one's self-esteem and to replace what's lacking in interpersonal relationships. Using money to get respect is an attempt to make up for the affection and self-confidence not forthcoming from strong relationships with other people. Certainly our consumer society encourages us to equate money with good feelings about ourselves.

If you find yourself comparing people, including yourself, to others based upon money, you may be trapped by the financial fallacy of money saying that people like you.

Financial Fallacy #4: Power

Power is the freedom to act without constraints placed on us by other people. Having power means that you are in control because you are stronger. In financial terms, power means having enough money to completely assert your will. Living according to this financial fallacy implies that you see life as an ongoing series of conflicts between what you want and what someone else wants, and that while you may choose to compromise, you will never lose in these conflicts if you have the most money.

When money is power, it means that having financial control is the same as having control over people and circumstances. It means that you can prevent unpleasantness in your life. This fallacy typically arises from a past that included the pain of humiliation and feelings of weakness. To escape those feelings, people attach themselves to money in an effort to become in charge, dominant, and self-reliant. No matter what, you will have the upper hand.

If you believe that with less money you have less control of your life, then you may be trapped by the financial fallacy of money that says "I am in charge of my life."

Seeking power is seeking control, yet we are not ultimately in control. We cannot control our lives. Our health (and that of our family), job conditions, and major economic factors control us all. Ultimately God the Creator has final say on what we have (even though we do and should participate through work).

Ironically, the Scriptures indicate that the way to exercise great power over others is not to rule over people, but to serve them.[1] Money's greatest power is unleashed when we use it cooperatively rather than competitively.

Financial Fallacy #5: Security

This fallacy tells us that there is some amount of money that can protect us from harm, prevent catastrophe, and give us a safe harbor to insulate us from life's storms. The insurance industry could not exist without this belief, and like all the others, this fallacy does have some basis of fact. Certainly there is wisdom in setting aside money "for a rainy day," and there is peace of mind in knowing that you can handle future needs even when they can't be well-defined in the present. King Solomon said, "A prudent person foresees the dangers ahead and takes precautions; the simpleton goes blindly on and suffers the consequences."[2]

Still, it can be unhealthy to worry about a future that's out of our hands and about events that are out of our control. Money as security becomes a financial fallacy when there is more than a normal desire for stability, characterized by a pervasive pattern of worrying about money.

Belief in money as security is generally an escape from past disappointments of being let down. The fallacy leads us to believe that with enough money, unmet expectations can be avoided and uncertainty in life eliminated. Money becomes a substitute for the support of other people, something that will always be there even if nobody else comes to the rescue. With money, you can take care of yourself and not have to rely on other people who may not be dependable.

If you are living with the financial fallacy of security—money says that you will always be safe—you probably have a pessimistic outlook on life that says your financial future will be negatively impacted by forces outside of your control. However, this fatalistic view of the future is stealing your joy in the present. The way to avoid such fatalism is to believe that a loving God will care about your welfare and can sustain you through rough times. Pain and suffering, like death and taxes, are certainties for rich and poor alike. The only way to feel safe against forces out of your control is to know that God controls all the forces. Our American coinage got it right: "In God we trust." If we want to feel secure, we must trust in a divine sovereign.

Financial Fallacy #6: Happiness

Give the money god your money in exchange for the pleasure he will bestow, our society says. Mark Twain was humorous, honest, and no doubt correct about many of us when he said, "I'm opposed to millionaires, but it would be dangerous to offer me the position."[3] The advertisers with their colorful, sensual commercials tell us money brings pleasure. That if we wear the right clothes, drive the right car, use the right credit card, tour the right vacation spots, read the right magazines, and on and on, we'll be abundantly, amazingly, astonishingly—and probably asininely—happy.

At my seminars, I often ask how many people believe that money buys happiness. Very few, if any, raise their hands. Then I ask how many people would like to have more money. First, many hands go up, and then the room breaks out in wry laughter when everybody realizes they've been trapped. It's nonsensical to want more money if money doesn't buy happiness!

You, too, may be guilty of the financial fallacy of money that says that I enjoy myself if you believe that with more money you would have a happier, more fulfilled, more contented life.

Clearly, happiness and contentment are things that money cannot buy. Surveys of money and happiness bear this out, as do the words of the wisest king of early Israel. As the ruler of one of the world's greatest empires, Solomon had greater wealth than all the kings of the world. All the world's rulers, including the famed Queen of Sheba, sought an audience with Solomon to glean from his wisdom, and they showed their admiration with lavish gifts.[4]

In spite of having everything he ever desired, near the end of his life he concluded that his wealth was a source of harm rather than happiness. The more he had, the more he wanted, so he never found the happiness he was seeking.[5] As he reflected on his accomplishments, he discovered that companionship, loving relationships, serving others and obeying God are the true currency of happiness. Without these things, he observed, life is meaningless.

THE UNIVERSAL FINANCIAL FALLACY

Possibly the most widely held financial fallacy is that "the grass is greener on the other side of the fence." Like the other fallacies, it is true enough to be credible. There is some fence somewhere surrounding greener grass than yours. But it is worse than the other fallacies because it offers no relief. This fallacy continually gnaws at us no matter how much money we gather and spend to make it go away. Since you can't own all the grass, there is always going to be someone with more of whatever it is you're trying to use money to get.

From the popularity of the TV show *Lifestyles of the Rich and Famous* to our fascination with the "Forbes 100 Richest Americans," we have an endless enchantment with how much money other people have. It's as if "love thy neighbor's wealth" has become the new golden rule.

But looks are deceiving and the financial fallacy of the grass is greener on the other side of the fence is the biggest deceit of all. At first glance, our neighbor's financial houses often look good, but a closer look would not be so inviting. Why? Because if we looked more closely, we'd find that money hasn't brought them the good life after all; their—and our—unmet emotional needs must be satisfied with something other than money.

Looking for the greener, brighter grass is the sin of comparison, with a bit of envy thrown in. The tenth commandment warns against covetousness. It is a wise and loving commandment, a divine protection against envy, a highly toxic emotion that "rots the bones."[6] Envy leads to the comparison trap, an endless cycle of reaching the top of one frame of reference, only to find yourself at the bottom of another. When you envy another's possessions, you give away the right to enjoy your own, denying yourself a pleasure that is a gift from God.[7]

You may be driven by the financial fallacy that the grass is greener on the other side of the fence if:

- you feel envious whenever you see a neighbor with a new car, or other major purchase;

- you avoid talking about financial matters for fear that you would feel inferior;

- you feel the need to keep up with what other people around you have; or

- you find yourself saying or thinking, "I wish I/we could have enough money to buy *(name of item)* like *(name of person who just spent money on it)."*

FINDING FREEDOM
FROM FINANCIAL FALLACIES

Get Wisdom

Many of these financial fallacies have noble ends—achievement, respect, security, happiness. But this is a case where the ends do not justify the means. Financial fallacies are lies, and they cannot coexist with a life of integrity, sincerity, honesty, or faith. These lies entrap us in potentially destructive behaviors that will cost us emotionally and cheat us financially.

The philosophy behind financial fallacies is "mind over matter." To become successful with money, though, one must have a philosophy of "wisdom over foolishness." If you are caught in a trap of erroneous beliefs about what money can do for you, then as King Solomon said, "Get wisdom. Though it cost all you have, get understanding." After all, "Of what use is money in the hand of a fool, since he has no desire to get wisdom?"[8]

The initial remedy for all financial fallacies is wisdom, the foundation of which is to honor, respect, and listen to God. When we choose to seek His goals, embrace His values, and meditate on His ways, our attitudes and actions will be protected against deceitful beliefs.

How do you escape the traps of financial fallacy? First, seek wisdom as described above. Second, consider yourself in relation to these fallacies; candidly assess which of them apply to you. Look honestly at each of the financial fallacies described in this chapter and ask yourself: What financial fallacies are a part of my life? How have they affected the ways that I have managed my money?

Practice Reframing

Next, practice reframing. This is a helpful way to apply wisdom—the best means to the best ends. *Reframing* is a fancy word professional counselors use to describe how we can change a negative statement into a positive one by changing its frame of reference. Financial fallacies keep us trapped within limiting and potentially harmful attitudes, but godly wisdom can provide us with new attitudes that are healing. In terms of financial fallacies, this can happen in one of two ways.

First, you can take a financial fallacy or a bad behavior associated with it, and see how that fallacy would be a good belief in another setting. This is called *context reframing*, taking an undesirable behavior with its disadvantages and seeing how that same behavior would have advantages.

For example, Lisa's parents believed in the fallacy that money is power. They taught Lisa the fallacy that money is bad. As missionaries, her parents labored in countries where the disparity between the wealthy and the poor was great. In addition, they had little money themselves, which only intensified their beliefs that "bad" rich people were causing financial hardship for "good" poor people. No wonder Lisa agreed with her parents that money is power, and that this power is always used negatively to hurt other people.

Lisa later went to work for a religious organization where she became friends with the development director who sought funds to support the organization's mission from wealthy individuals. Then she began to see that there were "good" rich people and came to change her perception about the financial fallacy of money as "bad" power. By reframing her perceptions, she saw that money could be used to accomplish good. Eventually, once freed from the deceit that money is bad, she was able to feel good about using her considerable skills to take on highly paid consulting work.

The second type of reframing is *content reframing*, in which you find a different meaning for the fallacy or behavior. For example, if you currently believe that money says you enjoy yourself, stop and think about what your favorite activities are. How much does it cost to take part in those activities? Most people are very surprised to find out they already have the money to make themselves happy!

Another example of reframing is changing the financial fallacy of security: Money says that I will always be safe. You could apply context reframing by recognizing how rich and poor alike are subject to the variations of life and seeing wealth as an opportunity to enjoy life in the present rather than worry about the future. Or you could apply content reframing by understanding what truly makes people secure. You are giving a new meaning to the word *secure,* a meaning that no longer can be satisfied by money. For instance, you begin to recognize that emotional connectedness in significant relationships will make you secure now and in the future. You conclude that relationships and lack of isolation, not money, are the keys to security.

We all perceive things and decide whether they are good or bad. Reframing changes our behaviors either by changing our perception (context) of situations or changing their interpretation (content). Either way, our behavior can change dramatically. Reframing is key to changing financial fallacies since they are based upon either poor perception or poor interpretation.

True wealth does not come from having enough money to buy achievement, freedom, respect, security, happiness, or power. Real wealth is a choice to use whatever money you have on things that you know make you happy that are already within your present affordability. It was Benjamin Franklin who insightfully said, "The more a man has, the more he wants. Instead of its filling a vacuum, it makes one." As opposed to financial fallacies, the truth about money is that real wealth lies in being content with less rather than hungering for more.

FINAL THOUGHTS ON FINANCIAL FALLACIES

Many of us probably feel like the champion boxer Joe Louis when he said, "I don't like money actually, but it quiets my nerves."[9] What makes financial fallacies so appealing is that they provide us with relief from emotional discomfort. However, a truer statement of the power of money comes from Benjamin Franklin, who said, "Money never made a man happy yet, nor will it. There is nothing in its nature to produce happiness."[10]

It is imperative that we understand the true nature of what money is. It is merely an economic tool that we use to satisfy our inner needs. Money is not achievement, freedom, respect, security, happiness, or power. These are deceitful and dangerous half-truths that lead us to use money in dysfunctional ways that may appease us in the short term but provide no lasting contentment, fulfillment, or satisfaction.

Let's hear again from the wealthiest man ever, King Solomon, who had this shrewd advice: "The man who knows right from wrong and has good judgment and common sense is happier than the man who is immensely rich! For such wisdom is far more valuable than precious jewels. Nothing else compares with it."[11]

CHAPTER FOUR

Money and Self-Esteem

> He is most powerful who has power over himself.
>
> —*Seneca*

It's nice to meet you, Bill. What do you do?"

"I'm an engineer," replied Bill.

How many times have you begun a similar conversation? Isn't it odd how often we define ourselves by our careers, as if who we are is defined by our source of income? And if our sense of self-worth isn't determined by our job, then we define ourselves by other things: our college degree, where we live, the kind of house we live in, the model car we drive, and so on. But whatever frame of reference we use, our sense of self-worth is probably attached to money in some form or fashion.

It's been said, "Comparison is the root of all inferiority."[1] This is especially true when it comes to money matters. There will always be somebody "better" than you, with higher income, less debt, more assets, better investments, and so on. Not only is this a game you can't win, it's a game not even worth playing. Even so, it is around the age of seven that we first begin the dangerous pastime of critically comparing ourselves to others. From then, it's just a matter of time before money becomes part of the evaluation criteria.

MEASURING ONESELF BY MONEY

Money has long been one of the objective standards by which we measure both ourselves and our ability to achieve our own goals. Money is a quantifiable, measurable, and objective way to make comparisons. But how do you measure pride, satisfaction, contentment, happiness, and joy? These are the things most worth achieving, but unlike cars, furniture, clothes, and other material possessions, they don't have a price tag or market value.

Does the following statement describe your feelings about yourself? "I really like and accept myself just the way I am and feel good about myself. Although managing my money is challenging at times, and I don't always do the right thing or even always know what the best thing to do is, I am sure that whatever I do with money has very little affect on how I feel about myself."

If you can repeat this affirmation with honest conviction, your experiences with money are probably enjoyable, rewarding and overall successful—according to your own standards. Still, for a variety of reasons (like the financial fallacies we explored in the previous chapter), many people let fears about their ability to handle money satisfactorily affect their attitudes about themselves. In turn, such fears can produce negative behaviors that work against financial success. Ignoring bills, overspending, hoarding, and gambling on get-rich-quick schemes are but some of the signs of low self-esteem regarding personal finance.

What has been considered to this point is our financial self-concept, in other words, what we know about ourselves in relation to money. Self-esteem, as compared to self-concept, is how we evaluate what we know about ourselves. It is our own unique self-rating of how worthy we believe we are, how much significance we believe we have to others, and how much we think we are capable of.

In our materialistic culture, money commands attention and respect as a benchmark for success. Financial success becomes a form of self-validation, the answer to the vital question of, "What am I worth as a person?" Ultimately, we want self-worth, and we want—even demand—that our money make us feel good about ourselves.

That's what makes financial fallacies so attractive. They make us feel good about ourselves in situations that would otherwise make us feel uncomfortable. We buy into fallacies because we are trying to buy self-esteem. But the higher our self-esteem, the less likely financial fallacies would deceive, and the better equipped we would be to cope with the financial challenges of life.

Clearly our self-esteem has a major influence on our relationship with money. It affects whether we will tend to approach financial decisions with confidence or with apprehension. How we act with money is an unconsciously drawn self-portrait of who we see ourselves to be.

Certainly there is a lot more to the concept of self-esteem than simply how we handle money. But because so much of our life's energy is spent earning, spending, and thinking about money, it must follow that having a positive image of yourself with money will tend to increase your overall self-esteem. Proven success and demonstrated competence with money gives you tangible evidence upon which to base a high self-rating, thus reinforcing and strengthening your overall level of self-esteem.

FIVE FINANCIAL "PATHOLOGIES"

When we allow poor money decisions or damaging financial fallacies to affect our self-esteem, a financial pathology can result. Here are five common financial pathologies: (1) overspending, (2) hoarding, (3) using money to control others, (4) using money to gain approval, (5) an inability to receive money.

Using Money as a Substitute for Love

Pathology, which refers to an abnormality or deviation due to disease, may seem to be a strong word to use with regard to financial behavior. But just as the body will become diseased from lack of food or water, the soul will become sick due to a lack of love. The need for food and water are normal to our physical natures. The need for love is normal to our psychological nature. The abnormal withholding of love for long periods of time will cause our souls to become diseased. The ultimate root of financial fallacies and their associated behaviors, financial pathologies, is using money as a love substitute.

Unfortunately, money is no substitute for love at all. The desire for self-worth and yearning for love cannot be bought with money. Instead, it can arrive in the form of human love, which we all need, and a deeper spiritual love, which we all crave. Since our essence is spiritual, we yearn for divine love; the Scriptures indicate that God loves us and wants us to seek Him.[2] God's love is proactive, pursuing us, and being concerned with what is best for us. Money, on the other hand, is a seducer that abandons us after promising to give us worth. It leaves us with an empty feeling, yet its allure is such that we return to its false assurances again and again.

When we feel physical pain, it is common to take a pain reliever. Financial pathologies often are responses to unmet emotional needs, such as love. Just as taking aspirin doesn't eliminate the condition, though you no longer feel the pain, a financial fallacy may medicate emotional pain but still leave the wounds in place. For instance, the person who never received affirmation for any of his efforts as a child may find that affirmation as an adult in a high salaried job. Therefore, he becomes conditioned to associate money with achievement, though he still feels only partly affirmed.

For small wounds, physical or emotional, the medicating effects of a short-term pain reliever may be all that is needed to cope. But just like you can't expect to run on a broken leg, medicated though you may be, when the belief in a fallacy leads you deeper into a financial pathology, the effects can be destructive, not only to your finances but also to your soul. The following five pathologies clearly are harmful. Read about each and determine if you are practicing any of them.

1. Overspending

Do you believe that people with money have happier, more fulfilled, and more contented lives; or do you believe that "Everything would be all right, if I only had a little more money"? Overspending is a common reaction to feeling powerless or lacking control. This is way to establish the perception of control.

Overspenders have difficulty making financial plans because they either feel too confined or they have problems sticking to plans. As we'll see in part 2, certain kinds of personalities are predisposed to overspending. But this pathology is also an unhealthy reaction to dealing with the stress of feeling out of control. It is quite common for children who lived with chemically dependent, abusive, miserly, or highly disciplinary parents to compensate by becoming overspenders. Children of overspenders are also likely to become overspenders themselves.

Do you avoid planning or keeping track of your finances? Do your spirits get a boost when you spend a lot of money? Do you find yourself shopping for no real need or reason other than just to shop? If any of these apply to you, you may struggle with overspending. If so, whenever you feel the urge to spend money, ask yourself why. Is there a real need to do so or are you feeling emotionally unsettled about something and needing to spend money to deal with it? You may even try keeping a journal, writing about your state of mind and emotions whenever you go shopping. You may uncover certain patterns of behavior that connect your feelings to your spending. Go back to chapter 2 and explore your money memories and see if you can locate the source of the urges to overspend.

2. Hoarding

Are you worried about not having enough money saved for the future? Do you judge people who spend a lot of money for present pleasures and short-term goals as being unwise and shortsighted? If overspending represents one extreme form of financial behavior, hoarding lies at the other end of the spectrum. Just as overspending is spending without legitimate reason, hoarding is oversaving without legitimate reason. The catalyst typically is fear of the future, and while certain kinds of personalities are predisposed to hoarding, the source is often a calamitous financial event from one's past.

Hoarding can be an emotional response to the unresolved pain of a past financial reversal. The goal is to secure control of one's future by accumulating enough money in the present to deal with any unexpected or unanticipated needs. It affects both pessimists, who are sure something bad is going to happen in the future, and optimists, who are sure that something good will happen as long as they have the funds available to take advantage of these presently unknown opportunities.

Oversavers should ask themselves many of the same questions that overspenders should ask, though the focus is on unnecessary saving rather than spending. Do you get unusual pleasure from planning or keeping track of your finances? Do you often worry about not having enough money for the future? Do you find yourself saving for no real need or future financial goal other than just to save more money? If any of these apply to you, you may struggle with hoarding. If so, ask yourself why. Go back to chapter 2 and explore your money memories and see if you can locate the source of the urges to hoard money.

3. Using Money to Control Others

Do you feel that having less money means having less power over people to live your life as your choose? Whereas some people have unspecified fears of the future, others have fears about people. Perhaps in the past they experienced great guilt or shame from failing to meet other's expectations. Having been conditioned to feel powerless about their own behavior, they try to fend off such feelings by controlling the behavior of others.

This is often seen in situations where a husband worries about his ability to be a good financial provider for his family. To avoid his feelings of inadequacy, he may exert domineering control over his wife's use of money and blaming her for everything that's "wrong"—real or quite often imagined—with their financial status. This control usually manifests itself in emotional pronouncements or accusations along the same theme: "You spend too much money! Don't you know how hard I'm working?"

Using money to control others is the result of projecting onto a person your fears that you may not measure up to the individual's expectations. It is a defense against experiencing the pain of rejection and the associated feelings of guilt or shame of letting down someone important to you. If you believe that money "makes the world go 'round" such that if you lose money, you will lose the power to accomplish your goals and feel in control of your life, you may struggle with this financial pathology. Go back to chapter 2 and explore your money memories and see if you can locate the source of the need to use money to control others. Because this pathology manifests itself in relationships, however, beware that others can only help you identify this pathology—and that requires you to relinquish enough control to accept their assessment of your financial behavior.

4. Using Money to Gain Approval

This pathology is a mirror image of using money to control others. Rather than restrict others' behavior to cope with feelings of inadequacy, this pathology uses money for others' benefit in order to "buy" their approval. It's natural to feel better about yourself when you make more money. Our society often operates as a meritocracy; that is, money is frequently the reward for a job well done. Therefore, it's easy to connect someone's payment for services rendered with the perception that they are also approving of you as a person.

But this tendency to think of money as approval can become a trap, especially for those who grew up experiencing little approval outside of what they merited through meeting someone's expectations. For example, children who always got money for good report cards or for doing household chores but received no affirmation for who they were as people were being conditioned to equate love with money. Also at risk are "latch-key kids" or children of busy parents who used gifts to make up for the lack of time spent in relationship. Receiving such gifts sets these children up for an adult lifetime of seeing others' money as an expression of love to them and them using money to express love to others.

Do you admire people who make a lot of money? Do you fear that people would look down on you if you suffered a loss of income for any reason? Why? Again, return to chapter 2 and explore your money memories and see if you can locate the source of the need to use money to gain the approval of others.

5. Inability to Receive

"No thanks. I don't need anything," is a frequent expression from those struggling with receiving from others. At least that's the verbalized version. What's often unsaid is, "I don't want anyone to think I need a handout." The inability to receive can affect everything from refusing the need for financial assistance to being able to truly enjoy receiving gifts that show affection. Not only does it frustrate the one who is trying to show affection but it further isolates the person from receiving the love that they and everybody else needs for healthy self-esteem.

Those who are critical of such responses usually say that "they're letting their pride get in the way," but I disagree. People who have difficulty receiving are letting their feelings of inadequacy get in the way. Sally, for instance is uncomfortable receiving gifts; her feelings came from an abusive childhood which led her to believe that she is not worthy of affection. Bryan, too, is a victim of an abusive, alcoholic father. He desperately would like to receive the loving expressions of others but fears that such affections would be short-lived. He's grown up believing that people are unreliable and can't be counted on for love, therefore it's better to go without than to be vulnerable to having that love snatched away from him. I also recall Neil, another adult who came to me for financial counsel. For Neil, a decline in his business created financial difficulties and made him feel like a poor provider for his family. Accepting financial assistance would only affirm his poor self-image.

Do you, too, struggle with receiving acts of kindness from others? Do you feel like every act of kindness shown you *requires* you to respond in like fashion? Do you run from the affection of others, or if you can't get away, find yourself feeling angry at them? These feelings may have financial implications. At a minimum, you may find yourself being a killjoy at holidays or birthdays. At worst, you may find yourself turning away needed financial assistance. The inability to receive is another financial pathology that may be just a minor distraction or an indication of deeply rooted emotional issues that could create major financial and emotional problems.

Behavior pathologies of all kinds are complex issues that defy simple diagnoses such as those offered here. However, lack of unconditional love is at the root of all of them. Unconditional love remains the greatest need of every person; often we receive love with strings attached. As a result, the emotions that drive financial pathology are typically fear (that another person will hurt you), guilt (from failing to do something good that was expected of you), or shame (from doing something bad that wasn't expected of you). For many people, these emotions amount to nothing more than financial headaches that can be medicated with small doses of financial fallacies or pathologies. Unfortunately, some will become addicted to money's pain-killing capacity and come to rely upon its short-term relief rather than seek long-term solutions. They will find that money is a poor substitute for love and eventually find themselves lacking both.

WHAT SHAPES OUR SELF-ESTEEM?

Your self-esteem is the result of your quest to find personal significance. How we perceive ourselves in relation to the world has a great impact on us. Given that, an understanding of what the world provides us as a frame of reference for self-esteem should be a critical part of the quest. Some of the determinants of self-esteem are the same factors that play such a major role in shaping our money personality. We will now revisit some of these elements to see their impact on our self-esteem, an important element of our money personality.

The many sociological factors that influence self-esteem are highly individualized, but they can be grouped in five areas; four external and one internal. The four external groups are:

- family of origin, which includes influences such as economic status, birth order, role models, family values, and traditions
- faith, which includes spiritual values and beliefs, and church community expectations
- peer group, which includes one's school and teachers, neighborhood, and workplace
- society, which includes cultural values generally transmitted through the media and gender stereotypes

The fifth area, innate personality, is an internal influence on self-esteem. Innate personality is our inner nature, an inborn pattern of attitudes and actions that we would manifest if there were no external influences.

65

Although we are generally unaware of it, our innate personality seeks approval from the external forces. Our behavior from an early age is often a response to the external pressures that try to force us to conform. A full discussion of each of these factors in relationship to self-esteem is beyond the scope of this book. But as you consider each of these factors, think about to what degree they have played a part in your own sense of self-worth as it relates to financial matters.

1. Family of Origin

Your family of origin or other early caregivers offered your first pictures of relationships and your model of love, sacrificial care, comfort, and encouragement. Even in your adulthood, the messages and values imparted through them can be an added source of strength against the other forces or a source of added pressure to your inner self.

In terms of money, your family's expectations regarding financial achievement will be an important reference point. For some, the only real expectation that was encouraged was to work diligently at whatever you love; this will tend to boost self-esteem. For others, the high expectations of their family in terms of career choice, income level, and lifestyle became (and may remain) sources of negative pressure on self-esteem.

2. Faith

Self-esteem issues related to finances and faith are complex, in that they represent an interweaving of the material and the immaterial. Because of the great differences that exist in terms of how people express their faith, the confluence of beliefs about faith and finance offer many opportunities for self-comparison.

The message of Jesus of Nazareth and the Christian faith regarding money can be summarized in one sentence: "You cannot serve both God and Money."[3] A succinct message to be sure, but the dilemma in applying this message is shaping a lifestyle that demonstrates service to the right master. Most people either implicitly or explicitly, practice one of three approaches to their financial spending:

1. Asceticism—a belief that money is evil and godly people are poor; therefore, self-denial is a measure of personal spiritual discipline;
2. Prosperity—a belief that money is a right and godly people are rich; therefore, wealth is the proper reward for obedience to God's Word;
3. Stewardship—a belief that money is a responsibility and godly people are trustworthy managers of God's resources.

If we are honest, we will admit that we attach a sense of self-righteousness to our particular view of faith and finance, and that this self-righteousness is an important aspect of our self-esteem. Depending on how visible your beliefs are, you are bound to experience some conflict with the differing beliefs of your family, coworkers, or culture in general, over the expression of your faith in your material lifestyle.

There may also be differences between your lifestyle and the lifestyle expectations within your community of faith. As with family, the messages and values imparted through one's faith can either be a source of great comfort through conformity or great pressure from the fear or guilt of nonconformity.

3. Peers

During elementary school we made the first serious comparisons of ourselves to the outside world. Most of us first faced competition in the classroom, and had ourselves objectively rated against others. There we also formed opinions of ourselves based upon subjective factors such as appearance, athleticism and, of course, material possessions. It's in those early peer group comparisons that we first learned about rich and poor, and which one we see ourselves as.

School was also the first time most of us dealt with differences in race and gender, differences that have their own financial connotations based upon one's perspective. We have often compared ourselves with others during almost 14,000 hours spent in school over twelve years. Self-doubts arose that may have affected our self-esteem throughout life.

4. Society

Whether the messages we receive about ourselves from family, faith, and peers are confirmed or rejected by society is a major influence on our self-esteem. This is probably the most pervasive influence of all on our financial self-esteem since it's society's money that we will earn and society's goods that we will consume.

If there is one basic message that could characterize American culture, it's probably the one captured in the popular bumper sticker of the 1980s: "He who dies with the most toys wins." In fact the 14,000 hours of schooling received by American children is offset by the 360,000 ads the typical teenager has seen by the time of their graduation, all telling them to buy.[4]

Many of these ads are seen on the primary source of cultural information—the television. By the time they finish high-school, U.S. children will have spent more time watching television than attending school.[5] This is problematic, as studies show that the buying patterns of those around us determine what we buy. Television, by instantaneously exposing millions of us to a common lifestyle, give each of us a national reference we can compare our local peers to. And generally, that lifestyle is beyond the level that most of us can afford.

Furthermore, the lifestyles portrayed on television shows and the products advertised during the programs are carefully designed to appeal to specific groups of people. Our financial self-esteem is sure to be influenced in some way by the extent that we have or do not have the lifestyle that TV producers and sponsors believe our demographic group is supposed to have.

Most troublesome of all are the cultural stereotypes that are propagated and preserved through the media. The stereotypical images given by media can personally and profoundly influence self-comparisons and ultimately lifestyle choices. Both television and print media consistently portray African-Americans, Latinos, and Hispanics less frequently than their representation in the population, and less financially successful than their actual achievements would merit.

Finally, there are significant societal expectations regarding the roles of men and women. Forty years of women increasing as part of the work force has made slow inroads into the societal stereotypes regarding men, women, and money. However, these stereotypes are so ingrained in our culture that products, advertising, and store layouts are designed to take advantage of them. Typically we feel self-affirmed when our financial behavior marches the norms about our sex.

Here are some of the most pervasive societal expectations men encounter regarding money:

- Men should be the family's primary breadwinner and therefore are expected to know how to handle money. Many men struggle to meet this expectation, due to both the growing equality of women in the workplace and the fact that few men are taught to be effective personal money managers.

- Men are supposed to be competitive; therefore their worth is measured by how much they earn, what type of work they do, and how financially successful they are. Because men do tend to approach life and relationships in a "one-up," or "where am I in the pecking order?" fashion more than women, this belief receives much real-life validation.

- Men are supposed to be independent, so if they don't know how to handle money, they are still not supposed to show weakness or ask questions for fear of losing face.

- Men are supposed to be more pragmatic about money. Therefore, while women "buy stuff," men just "shop" for something specific. In other words, women are gatherers, but men are hunters. Also, retailers believe that women shop to fulfill fantasies, while men shop for the sake of utility. Although these characterizations may be simplistic, there is evidence that validates this expectation. As we'll see in chapter 5, men's personalities tend to be more pragmatic and it shows in their shopping habits. Only 31 percent of mall shoppers are men, and when they do go, they spend less time and money in malls than women.[6]

Because men do tend to sustain these cultural norms by their own behavior, those messages are significant forces, positive or negative, to a man's self-esteem. One study found that three of the most important factors contributing to men's self-esteem related to work or power.[7] Whether it's the Wall Street deal makers or entertainment superstars, society highly values the hard-driving, deal-making, financially successful male who uses his success and acumen to achieve a conspicuously consumerist lifestyle. Likewise, men with nontraditional male interests such as arts and crafts or gardening may be regularly questioned as to why they aren't into sports or home electronics. The stay-at-home Mr. Mom, the public servant, the minister or school teacher will have a much harder time finding affirmation for his role in society. Some men find themselves pursuing such careers later in life after they've found that the career choices they made based upon societies expectations were unfulfilling.

If you are a woman, here are some of the most pervasive societal expectations you face regarding money:

- Women are supposed to be financially provided for and not supposed to know much about money. The statement seems so derogatory and narrow-minded that it's hard to take seriously or without offense. Yet look at the many ways our society affirms this norm, among them the inequality of women's salaries for equivalent work; the "glass ceiling" preventing entrance into the executive ranks of business; the expectation that working moms are still to be the primary caretaker of the home; and in major financial transactions such as a car or house, the relatively condescending treatment women receive as opposed to the deferential treatment men receive, even by women salespeople.

- Women are cooperative, and therefore will adjust their behavior to be accommodative rather than competitive, to be "one-down" rather than "one-up" in order to maintain relational harmony. This cooperative nature is often reflected in their desire for intimacy rather than independence.

- Women are emotional "feelers" instead of pragmatic "thinkers," and this, too, is seen in their shopping habits, where compared to men, they show a greater concern for the welfare of others, are much more spontaneous, much

70

more social and seek buying information from other people more often.

Women who don't fit the societal norms suffer from lack of validation just as nonconforming men do. Many women grow up hearing messages that they need to select a career that will enable them to stay at home with children and that some careers, such as those related to math and science, are not appropriate for women.[8] Still, in many ways, women's own behavior validates the relevance, if not necessarily the correctness, of these beliefs. The same self-esteem survey referred to above found that women rated physical attractiveness as important a source of self-esteem as work. Thus, the retailers assumption that women buy to fulfill fantasies is affirmed by women's own beliefs and behaviors.

The danger inherent in society's gender norms is that those who don't fit suffer the consequences of being arbitrarily assigned a lower status. A woman or man who feels the lower status often experiences isolation, guilt, shame, and ultimately low self-esteem. When the violated norms relate to one's financial status, people usually turn to destructive financial fallacies or financial pathologies for relief from the inevitable stresses of being considered outside the boundaries of acceptability.

THE ROLE OF INNATE PERSONALITY

Many factors influence behavior: upbringing, economic background, cultural expectations, religious beliefs, role models, friends, and specific life circumstances. Although these influences affect and may, to a degree, shape our behavior, in most situations we will react with a set of automatic responses. We will react in ways that make us the most comfortable, according to our inner nature.

That inner nature is our inborn personality, a pattern of genetically predetermined behavioral tendencies. As we grow from childhood, through adolescence and into adulthood, we develop consistent patterns of attitudes and actions in response to the everyday demands of life. We begin to prefer certain responses because they feel natural to us and a lifetime of financial decisions gives us many opportunities to exhibit these innate tendencies.

Like most parents, I am fascinated at the natural differences between our two daughters. Even though they are young, I am especially impressed at how different they are when it comes to money. Our ten-year-old is a money-saving, window-shopping, coupon-clipping planner who turns out lights and shuts off faucets to conserve money. Our seven-year-old is an instant-gratification, money's-burning-a-hole-in-her-pocket shopper. Rather than save what she has, she seeks ways to earn more. Neither approach is right or wrong. Both are expressions of their innate personalities in the financial realm, and the more that we understand about our own inborn personality characteristics, the more we will appreciate our individual uniqueness, improve our self-knowledge, and increase our self-esteem. (We will look at this more in part 2.)

Each of these four forces of family, faith, peers, and society are interdependent and interrelated, and they act powerfully. As these external forces act on our inner nature, they, too, become a part of who we are. Whether they become a good part or bad part depends upon the degree to which our innate personality finds itself in accord or conflict with the external forces attempting to influence it. Our self-esteem, then, is in a constant state of refinement as it is shaped by our internal responses to the external forces.

Comprehending the nature and scope of these forces in our own lives is critical to self-knowledge. Self-esteem begins with self-knowledge, accepting ourselves as we are and having a willingness to make the most of what we have been given. The more we can learn about ourselves, the better we can successfully manage ourselves, as we will tend to set goals that are appropriate for us as unique individuals.

Attaining these self-determined goals leads to increased competence and success, which contributes to greater feelings of worthiness and higher self-esteem. And the higher our self-esteem, the better equipped we are to cope with the challenges of life, especially in the financial arena.

Still, knowledge of the factors that influence us is only the beginning. The truth is that we often use our net worth not to buy self-worth but to protect it, to avoid the pain of unmet emotional needs caused by being overpowered against our will or our nature by the outside pressures. But the irony is that our efforts to protect ourselves are often self-destructive.

For example, if you had a bad day at the office you might buy something just because "I deserve it." If you're guilty about ignoring your family, you might buy presents to make up for the lost time. If you're feeling poor, you might charge a large purchase to feel rich, and if you're feeling selfish, you might make a large donation to feel more benevolent.

But money deceives. It cannot buy any of these things. While our self-esteem may get a boost in the short-run, eventually it falls because all we've done is conform to the expectations of others rather than find value in our own uniqueness. Ultimately, all financial fallacies say the same thing, that our net worth can tell us about our self-worth.

PART TWO

Your Personality and Money

CHAPTER FIVE

You've Got Personality

A man's mind is the man himself.

—Latin Proverb

Pete calls himself "frugal," but his family and friends say he is a "tightwad." He has a number of money rules that he strictly lives by, like, "Don't go into debt"; "Paying interest is such a waste of money"; and "Always save for a rainy day." With a family to support, Pete takes his financial responsibilities very seriously—too seriously, according to his wife, who wishes he would loosen up his grip on the family finances. He keeps a budget, tracks every expense and, if necessary, will go without things to be ready for anything, "just in case."

Pete is very concerned about the future—retirement ("Social Security isn't going to be there"), college tuition ("it's a tough job market and our kids need to be prepared") and the financial crisis he is sure is looming on the horizon. The stock market? Forget it—too risky. Safe, secure government bonds, bank CDs and their nearly paid-off home are all Pete trusts. Safety and security is what Pete values and money is the perfect tool to attain his goals. He thinks most people are irresponsible when it comes to money and can't understand why people don't take money as seriously as he does.

Suzy, on the other hand, calls herself "fun-loving" and a "free spirit" but others think she's "out of control" and a "wild woman." Suzy lives according to financial "rules" also: "Easy come, easy go. There's always more where that came from!" and "Nothing ventured, nothing gained!"

The last thing Suzy thinks of in terms of money is saving it. There's too much fun to be had spending it and the sooner it's spent, the better. Budget? "Who has time for that? And what's the point? If you want something you don't have the money for, just use plastic!" she says, as she proudly displays her fifteen credit cards, all well on their way to being maxed out. Suzy knows she'll have to get serious about her finances someday. Still, Suzy thinks that most people are too uptight about money and can't understand why they take money so seriously.

How would you respond if Suzy was your kid sister or Pete was your brother-in-law? One of the most valuable skills we can have is the ability to understand what motivates us and influences our behavior—and that of those we care for. People are different for many reasons, including genetic makeup, parental influences, life circumstances, social customs. What motivates one person will have no effect on another. As the saying goes, "One's man's meat is another man's poison."

Since so much of our behavior is consumed by thoughts and actions involving money, understanding our motivations and influences is critical to our success in managing our personal finances.

THE POWER OF YOUR PERSONALITY TYPE

Like Pete and Suzy, all of us have identifiable and even predictable patterns of behavior. We each have an inborn, natural personality, a behavioral road map that leads us to act in certain automatic ways. *Personality type* is one method of describing these normal ways of doing things. Similarities and distinctions between people can be easily understood within the framework of personality types. While we have explored other external factors influencing our money personality, such as parents, peers, and culture, it's personality type that causes us to approach most financial situations with a preferred course of thought and set of responses that come most naturally to us.

Knowing your personality type is fundamental to understanding your behavior. It is your essential nature, the most basic way to describe you and all of your human resources, strengths and weaknesses. In addition, personality type can explain why certain styles of communicating or accomplishing tasks work for some people and not for others. Being aware of personality type can improve self-management skills as well as enhance the productivity of people at work and their effectiveness in interpersonal relationships. As a management tool, personality type has benefited managers by helping them identify the strengths and weaknesses of project and work teams.

A long-recognized tool for describing personality type is the Myers-Briggs Type Indicator®, or MBTI™.[1] It's an effective way of understanding ourselves and others. There are, of course, many ways to determine personality type, but few are as useful, far-reaching and fun as the MBTI. After 50 years of research and development, it has become the leading instrument for understanding normal personality differences. More than two million indicators are administered each year in the United States and it has been translated into more than 30 languages as well.

INTRODUCTION TO THE
MYERS-BRIGGS TYPE INDICATOR

The Myers-Briggs Type Indicator was developed by the mother-daughter team of Katherine Cook Briggs and Isabel Briggs Myers. Both had a life-long zeal for understanding different types of personalities. Isabel, in particular, was driven by a desire to find a way for people to understand rather than destroy each other. She was also especially interested in helping people find jobs that they were tempermentally suited for.

Isabel Myers viewed personality type as a gift from God, one to be cherished and valued for its innate ability to make unique contributions to society. Moreover, she believed that personality type was extremely useful in improving communications among people and that differences, once appreciated, would be mutually constructive in relationships.

FOUR PERSONALITY DIMENSIONS

The indicator is based upon four dimensions of our personalities:

1. how we prefer to gather information: through observing facts and details *or* by envisioning patterns and possibilities;

2. how we prefer to make decisions: on the basis of logic and objective considerations *or* personal values;

3. where we prefer to direct our energy: to the outer world of activities and spoken words *or* the inner world of thoughts and ideas; and

4. how we prefer to orient ourselves to the external world: in a structured, planned way, knowing where we stand *or* in a flexible, adaptable way, discovering new things as we go.

Each dimension is a key aspect of life, which makes it easy to see why these aspects are so accurate in explaining and predicting your own and others' behavior. Although it is true that, depending on the situation, we may act in ways consistent with any of these preferences, we do not use each preference with equal frequency, interest, intensity, or success. In each of the four dimensions, everybody will tend to use one preference more than the other.

Personality Types: A Matter of Preference

A good example of this is the handwriting activity that is a popular exercise in MBTI workshops. You can try it now. Find a piece of paper and write your name on it. How did that feel? That's actually a hard question for most people to answer because you don't think enough about writing your name to easily describe how it feels. You just do it.

Now write your name in your nonwriting hand. Notice how hard it is to even get the pen to feel comfortable enough in your hand to get started. How did that feel? Awkward? Clumsy? Difficult? Weird? Compare the quality of the two results. It is extremely rare that the writing of the nondominant hand is anywhere near the quality of that produced by the preferred hand.

This exercise demonstrates the concept of preference and is an analogy for personality type. Although you can write with your nonpreferred hand, it requires more thought and effort; it takes longer and is more tiring; and the results are not nearly as satisfactory. Likewise, when working with our personality preferences, life is easier, more enjoyable, less stressful, and more productive. We are simply more talented and gifted when operating according to our personality type.

The MBTI model says that each of us has our own set of preferences for thoughts and actions, and while we are not constrained to just that set (just as we are not constrained to always writing using our dominant hand), we will generally be at our best when we are using our preferences. Because we are good at using our preferences, we use them with confidence, which typically produces good results, which then reinforces our tendency to use them and causes their repeated use. This is desirable, because all personality types are equally good even though different in their approaches to life, and everybody benefits when we are "on our best behavior."

We use one set of preferences primarily but not exclusively. Our preferences are unconscious innate tendencies, and while you may choose to override that tendency and operate outside your preference, it does not change your inborn preference or personality type. The degree of conformity and consistency to our type will be affected by other genetic differences and the pervasiveness of external forces such as birth order, upbringing, education, life circumstances, and socioeconomic background.

In addition, people of similar personality type will differ in the strength of their preferences. Still, it is remarkable how much people of the same type have in common. Therefore, it can be said that you are a lot like, somewhat like, and not at all like people with your same personality type.

WHAT'S MY TYPE?

The MBTI is a scientifically developed psychological instrument administered by trained, qualified professionals. Decades of research have shown that it is the most reliable and valid method for determining your personality preferences. If you have never taken the MBTI, this section can help you make an informal, yet informed appraisal of your preferences. You will have the opportunity to choose between the statements below (denoted A and B) in each of four dimensions, or categories, and then to determine your personality type.[2]

Extravert or Introvert

The first personality type dimension concerns itself with where people prefer to focus their energy each day, either around people, doing and saying things; or in private, introspective contemplation. We need to do both but *extraverts* prefer to direct their attention to the *outer* world of people, places, things, and activity. They receive energy and inspiration from crowds of people and things happening around them. *Introverts,* on the other hand, prefer to draw their attention inward, to the *inner* world of ideas and reflection where they can recharge themselves after expending energy on people and external things.

When extraverts and introverts are at a social function, the extraverts typically talk demonstratively but briefly with many people, are the last ones to leave, and return home charged up and wanting to talk about the event to unwind. By contrast, the introverts are talking quietly and in depth with a small group of people or just one at a time; they will leave early, feel drained, and will need time alone to recover their energy.

Consider the following statements then circle the preference in each pair that best describes you.[3]

A: I prefer to work around others.
B: I prefer to work by myself.

A: I prefer to work on several projects at a time.
B: I prefer to focus on one task at a time.

A: I usually act first, then think about it.
B: I usually think first, then act.

A: I am more of a public person.
B: I am more of a private person.

The first statement in each pair typifies the extravert; the second typifies the introvert. Extraverts tend to prefer working around other people and like exchanging information and receiving input from others. They tend to be generalists who prefer variety, action, and breadth—knowing a little about a lot of things. In contrast, introverts prefer to work in solitude and find interruptions distracting. Introverts tend to be specialists who prefer constancy, concentration, and depth—knowing a lot about a few things.

Extraverts respond quickly: do-think-do. Meanwhile, introverts defer action: think-do-think. While an extravert would say, "Shoot first, then ask questions later," an introvert would say, "Don't shoot until you see the whites of their eyes." An extravert's approach is, "It's easier to ask forgiveness than ask permission," while an introvert's approach is "Haste makes waste."

Extraverts like to communicate by talking. They are comfortable thinking out loud, offering opinions quickly, and don't mind drawing attention to what they are saying or doing. Introverts would rather communicate in writing. They find out what they think by going inside of themselves, offer opinions after a time of contemplation, and guard their privacy.

Recent data suggests that the U. S. population is equally divided between extraverts and introverts.[4] You probably have a fairly clear idea of whether you are an extravert or introvert. If not, look at your circles above to see if three or all four are A (or B). You also can ask someone who has observed you in a variety of settings to suggest your preference. If you are an extravert, mark an *E* on the first of the four spaces in the box "My Type Is" on page 90. If you are an introvert, mark an *I* on the first space of "My Type Is. . . ."

Sensor or Intuitive

The next preference deals with how people take in, or perceive, information. It is vital in terms of interpersonal relationships because it is the starting point for nearly all that we do. If two people cannot agree on what they see in the same situation, some amount of conflict is probably unavoidable.

Do you see the details or seek the big picture? Sensors, those with a preference for sensing, are very observant. Their thoughts are influenced by what they see, hear, smell, touch, and taste through the five senses. Their focus is on the immediate, real, practical facts of experience of life and how they can apply to the task at hand.

If you like to see the big picture, you probably are an intuitive. People with a preference for intuition almost instantly jump their minds to connections, relationships, and possibilities relating to their perceptions. Intuitives emphasize insight into the future. Their focus is on what the present reality means so that they can project what it can be rather than experience it as it is.

At a MBTI workshop I attended a few years ago, two groups of participants were asked to describe an apple. The sensing group identified the apple's features: green, round, hard, crunchy, tart, juicy. The intuitives, however, when asked what they thought about the same apple responded with: farmer's market, apple pie, applesauce, gift for the teacher, bobbing for apples, candied apples. Both groups were amazed and amused at the stark differences in perception about something as rudimentary as an apple.

Circle either A or B in each of the pairs as you consider which preference best describes you, sensing or intuition.

A: I prefer to pay more attention to the facts and details.
B: I prefer to try to understand the connections, underlying meaning, and implications.

A: I am a more down-to-earth and sensible person.
B: I am imaginative and creative.

A: I like new ideas only if they have practical uses.
B: I like new ideas just for their own sake.

A: I prefer to use an established skill.
B: I become bored easily after I have mastered a skill.
A: I prefer to rely on direct, personal experience or the experience of others.
B: I'm comfortable going with my "gut instinct" or "educated guess."

Looking at the above five pairs of statements, the differences between sensing and intuition should be clear. At work, sensors are quite content to focus on just their job, while intuitives enjoy their present assignment only to the extent that they can see it completing a necessary part of their overall career plans.

Meanwhile, sensing types tend to be more practical than intuition types, while intuitives tend to be more innovative.

A word about the pragmatic mind of the sensing person versus the creative mind of the intuition person. (Note the second set of statements above.) This has a direct implication on how each regards money. The sensor tends to find daydreaming a terrible waste of a mind and thinks that people who do daydream have too much time on their hands. When it comes to money, his attitude would be one of "waste not, want not." Intuitives not only daydream but fantasize about several things at once. They would rather dream about how to invest for retirement—and where they will retire to—and what they will do in retirement, than balance their checkbook.

Concerning personal experience, sensors work through the issues of the present by recalling what they learned from the past. (Sensors tend to view the future with suspicion.) Their experiences and those of others are important. In contrast, intuitives tend to see the past as generally irrelevant but find the future intriguing and exciting. What they do in the present is simply a part of where they see themselves going.

Sensing types represent about 65 percent of the U.S. population and intuition types about 35 percent.[5] You probably have a fairly clear idea of whether you are a sensor or an intuitive. If not, ask someone who has observed you in a variety of settings to suggest your preference. If you are a sensor, mark an S on the second of the four spaces in the box "My Type Is" on page 90. If you are an intuitive, mark an N on the second space.[6]

Thinker or Feeler

Thinking and *feeling* describe the two ways that people make judgments and arrive at decisions after they have perceived information. Thinkers prefer coming to conclusions in an objective and impersonal manner, relying on the logic and consistency of universal principles that can be applied in all situations. By contrast, feelers include personally held values and the needs of the people involved in their decision making. As opposed to the thinker who finds that treating everybody the same is "fair," feelers hold that fairness is doing whatever is needed on a case-by-case basis.

85

While thinkers can be regarded as detached and cold, and feelers as personally involved and tenderhearted, both can be very emotional. Thinkers feel, sometimes with great emotion, and feelers think. However, when it comes to making decisions, thinkers prefer to step outside their feelings to protect their objectivity, while feelers prefer to step into their feelings to assure themselves of acting according to their personal values or priorities.

The thinking-feeling personality dimension is one of the most difficult to ascertain because both preferences are very desirable and people tend to use both frequently. Still, nearly everybody has a definite preference on this dimension. Consider the following pairs of statements, then circle the letter that reflects the preference that best describes you.

> A: I prefer to settle disagreements based upon premises that are fair and objective even if it means that someone will be unhappy.
> B: I prefer to make decisions based upon what will create the most harmony.

> A: Generally I believe that a good end result can only be arrived at through a sound, logical reasoning process.
> B: Generally I believe that a good decision is one that has an end result of peace, harmony, and mutual acceptance irrespective of the process.

> A: People probably would call me logical and analytical.
> B: People probably would call me sensitive and empathetic.

> A: I prefer to solve issues by trying to put my emotions aside and step back to see the problem from the outside looking in.
> B: I prefer to solve issues by allowing my emotions to personally involve myself in the problem, seeing it from the inside looking out.

> A: I am very impressed by a cogent, logical, and well-crafted argument.
> B: I am very impressed by a forceful, passionate, and sincere emotional appeal.

Thinking types and feeling types are equally represented in the U.S. population, but this is the only preference with a distinct gender differentiation. Approximately two-thirds of men are thinkers and two-thirds of women are feelers.[7] Many of the easily observable behavior differences between men and women can be accounted for by the difference in thinking and feeling.

You probably have a fairly clear idea of whether you are a thinker or feeler. If not, ask someone who has observed you in a variety of settings to suggest your preference. If you are a thinker, mark a *T* on the third of the four spaces in "My type is . . ." on page 90. If you are a feeler, mark an *F* on the third space.

Judger or Perceiver

The final preference dimension relates to what kind of lifestyle people prefer: planned, organized and controlled, or spontaneous, flexible, and adaptable. A judger's natural drive is toward operating according to a structured system, deciding what to do, doing it, and moving on. A perceiver's natural drive is to keep plans and structure to a minimum so that they can readily respond to new information and change course, if necessary.

Once again, it is important to understand the meaning of each term within the context of the Myers-Briggs model. Judging does not imply that someone is judgmental. It means that they prefer to use a judging process—thinking or feeling—in their basic approach to life. In other words, judgers like to *decide,* and will use their deciding preference, thinking or feeling, to do so.

Likewise, perceiving does not mean that a person is unusually perceptive. It means that he prefers to use a perceiving process—sensing or intuition—in their approach to life. In other words, perceivers like to *gather information,* and will use their perceiving preference, sensing or intuition, to do so.

To see how planned and organized judgers are and how spontaneous and flexible perceivers are, I only need to observe people who attend my personality-type workshops. At every Myers-Briggs workshop the majority of judgers are early and relieved to be in place on time, while the perceivers are typically late yet quite casual about it. I recall one judger saying that the perceivers told time in "ish"—"I'll be over at 7-ish"—adding the "at" before the "ish," as if that conveyed an acceptable level of preciseness. What confounded him was the fact that perceivers always seemed to arrive on the after side of "ish," like 7:20, rather than the before side, like 6:55.

Consider the following statements that will help you determine which preference best describes you, judging or perceiving. Circle the letter that corresponds to your preference.

A: I prefer to have things settled and decided.
B: I prefer to leave my options open, just in case something else comes up.

A: I'm very conscious of time and consider being on time important.
B: I frequently run late, and yet, I feel relaxed about doing so.

A: People tend to notice how well organized I am and how everything seems to be in its proper place.
B: People tend to notice how disorganized I am and are amazed that I can ever find anything.

A: I feel better about completing my work before I can relax.
B: I often find reasons to stop what I'm doing so I can move on to something else.

Remember, perceivers like to keep open their options, judgers like things settled. It was Fred G. Sanford, from the popular TV show *Sanford and Son,* who said, "Don't put off until tomorrow what you can put off until the day after tomorrow!" As a perceiver, I have always found great humor—and personal truth—in that statement. Judgers, by contrast, are the ones who say (with a gleam in their eye, I might add), "Plan your work and work your plan!"

How organized are judgers and flexible (disorganized) are perceivers? At my workshops I find that the judgers not only have arrived early, but have their coats and personal items properly put away, their materials out, and are ready to get to work. Not only are the perceivers usually late, I find them often asking someone if they can borrow pens, paper, or even if they may share necessary materials that they forgot. Judgers typically have their filing cabinets neatly lined with well-marked folders, books filed on shelves, and few papers in their in box. Perceivers usually have everything stacked on their floor, desk, shelves, or in box (rarely does something ever get to the outbox) with no apparent system. But they always seem to know where everything is—until someone "does them a favor" by cleaning up for them.

The judging-perceiving difference is said to be the most frequent source of interpersonal conflict. Perceivers are stressed by feeling confined. They resist having their finances budgeted, their time scheduled, their desks neat and their work planned. Judgers are stressed by lack of boundaries. They find great comfort in their budgets, their day timers, their filing systems, and to-do lists.

Yet, it can also be a great source of positive interaction. For example, the senior pastor of a rapidly growing nondenominational church in Virginia has a judger's strong preference for structure, order, plans, and schedules. On the one hand, the operational efficiency of the organization is enhanced by his gift of providing systems and control. On the other hand, the needs and demands of a large congregation don't always fit into a predefined system. To that end, a position was created to handle the constant flow of unplanned interruptions, a position that fits his assistant's gifts of adapting to and handling the unexpected.

Judging types represent an estimated 60 percent of the American population and perceiving types the other 40 percent.[8] You probably have a fairly clear idea of whether you are a judger or perceiver from completing the above A/B preference exercise. If not, ask someone who has observed you in a variety of settings to suggest your preference. If you are a judger, mark a *J* on the last of the four spaces in the box below. If you are a perceiver, mark a *P* on the last space.

Exercise 6

YOUR PERSONALITY TYPE

Using the A/B statements and the descriptions of extravert/introvert, sensor/intuitive, thinker/feeler, and judger/perceiver from pages 82–89, place the appropriate letter for each of your personality-type dimensions in the corresponding blank below.

My Type Is . . .

____ ____ ____ ____

CELEBRATING YOUR TYPE

Congratulations! If you've completed "My Type Is . . ." and estimated your personality type, you have taken a meaningful step toward better self-awareness for better self-management. Soon we will consider how this knowledge will benefit your personal financial management. For now, it's crucial that you begin the process of understanding who you are before we move on to how to use this understanding for your financial benefit.

Now that you've estimated your type, refer to appendix 1 for more descriptions of each type. By reading the descriptive words associated with your estimated type, you should be able to validate your personality type. If you are unsure about one or two preferences, look at appendix 2, which shows each of the four pairs of preferences. Review the preferences that are in doubt, reading the appropriate descriptions. The keywords associated with each preference can help you verify a preference or resolve those still in doubt. If you are still undecided about one or two preferences, the next chapter on temperament may help you decide.

WHAT PERSONALITY TYPE IS . . . AND IS NOT

Personality type is an easy way of understanding yourself and others, in broadly accurate terms. It offers to us an easily accessible and self-affirming road map to greater self-awareness. In general, the personality type framework provides us with an excellent way to explain many of the observable patterns of normal human behavior.

While there are infinite forms of thought and action, understanding their pattern within the context of personality type provides us with an effective way to improve self-management, enhance personal growth and development, and enrich our interpersonal relationships. In the arena of personal finance, the concepts of personality type will help you manage your money in ways that are the most natural and beneficial to you.

Personality type is not a prescription for how to live. Instead, knowing personality type is having a tool for recognizing and understanding differences between people. There is no one best type to be. In using your type's natural assets, you will find great satisfaction in life, according to personality-type theory.

Personality type should not be used to put people into a box, in the negative sense of stripping people of their unique individual qualities. Human behavior is far too complex to be described by a single model, even one as accurate as the MBTI. Type is a way of categorizing people according to their talents and giftings, which will vary even among people of the same type. People who share similar personality types are a lot like each other, somewhat like each other, and not at all like each other.

In *Gifts Differing*, Isabel Myers wrote, "For most people, really understanding their own type in particular, and other people's types in general, is a releasing experience rather than a restrictive one. It sets one free to recognize one's own natural bent and to trust one's own potential for growth and excellence, with no obligation to copy anyone else, however admirable that person may be in his or her own different way."[9]

Personality type is not a mandate for behavior. While your innate personality type predisposes you to certain behaviors, it is not the cause. In addition to a personality, you were born with a free will which, depending on your circumstances, permits uninhibited expressions of thought and action.

Personality type does not determine how competent you will be, although it provides good clues for what things you may naturally be good at. Opportunity, education, practice, motivation, and desire work together with your personality to produce positive results.

Personality type is not an excuse for bad behaviors, poor performance, or a reason to avoid unpleasant tasks. We are all accountable for our actions—accountable to each other and ultimately to God.

Personality type does not place boundaries around your path to personal growth and development. Isabel Briggs Myers saw each of the sixteen types as different paths to excellence. Growing in the knowledge of your personality type can make your life, especially your financial life, more fruitful and meaningful.

CHAPTER SIX

What's Your Temperament?

Hide not your talents, they for use were made.
What's a sundial in the shade?

—*Benjamin Franklin*

To Dorothy there was no place like home. The Scarecrow could unravel every riddle if he only had a brain. The Tin Man would register emotion if he only had a heart. And with enough courage, the Lion would "trash a hippopotamus from top-to-bottomus."

Interestingly, these four beloved characters on their way to see the Wizard of Oz revealed desires we all have. Dorothy and her friends had the need for:

- a safe, secure place where you know you belong;
- great intellectual powers;
- the capacity to love and respond to affection; and
- the courage to overcome anything, no matter the odds.

Most people have all four of these desires; yet, as individuals, each of us has a drive to satisfy one above the others. This drive is our life's quest and like the quest of the seekers of the wizard, it defines us and impels all of what we say and do, and want from life.

In expressing their innermost needs and desires, Dorothy, Scarecrow, Tin Man, and Lion were manifesting the essential natures of four different behavior patterns that have been observed in human behavior for over 2500 years. In 450 B.C., Hippocrates discerned four dispositions that he called *temperament:*

the genial, lively, and impulsive *sanguine;* the self-sacrificing, sober, and emotionally sensitive *melancholic;* the imaginative, strong-willed, and passionate *choleric;* and the calm, cool and collected, reticent, and impersonal *phlegmatic.*

THE FOUR TEMPERAMENTS

Since that time, other philosophers, writers, psychologists, and clergy of different times and cultures have also observed four distinct natures that characterize people. For instance, Paracelsus in 1550 described the four temperaments as *changeable, industrious, inspired,* and *curious;* and as recently as 1947, Erich Fromm described the four temperaments as *exploitative, hoarding, receptive,* and *marketing.* No matter what names the commentators used to describe the four natures, their characterizations had remarkable similarities.[1] There is a consistent tendency for human behavior to set itself into four similar patterns of interrelated characteristics.

Exercise 7

YOUR TEMPERAMENT PATTERN

To determine your temperament pattern, recall from the end of chapter 5 your four-letter MBTI code, i.e. ISFJ or ENTP. Then do the following:

- If the second letter is an S (for sensor), go to the last letter of your MBTI code to complete your two-letter temperament code. Your code will be S and that letter. For example, if your MBTI code is ISFJ, your temperament code is SJ.

- If the second letter is an N (for intuitive), go to the third letter of your four-letter MBTI code to complete your two-letter temperament code. Your code will be N and that letter For example, if your MBTI code is ENTP, your temperament code is NT.

Complete this exercise now.

Four-letter MBTI code: __ __ __ __   Two-letter temperament code: __ __

To read your temperament code, use this legend:
SJ=melancholy, SP=sanguine, NF=choleric, NT=phlegmatic.

Before we proceed, determine your temperament by completing the simple exercise on the preceding page.

One observer of American culture has suggested that the landscape of the American soul has been imprinted by the disparate influence of four major groups, each configured around unique animating principles:

- Transcendents, spiritualists impelled by a transcendent, visionary, idealistic hope;
- Preservers, traditionalists, driven by a romantic longing to preserve the social forms of their Old European roots;
- Transformers, industrialists, inspired by the practical challenges of promoting social and material progress;
- Dissolvers, seekers of the primitive intensity and anarchic freedom-loving vitality of frontier life.[2]

Interestingly, and perhaps not coincidentally, the attitudes and behaviors of each of these groups conform to the classic temperament classifications. The energizing forces of the transcendents, preservers, transformers, and dissolvers, quite accurately correspond to those of the cholerics (NF), melancholics (SJ), phlegmatics (NT) and sanguines (SP), respectively. In addition, the observer of these American cultural groups further subdivides them into four subcultures for a total of sixteen types, once again conforming to the number of Myers-Briggs personality types.

Temperament is widely used in conjunction with the Myers-Briggs Type Indicator because temperament is a vital subset of type in that it provides the widest base of accurate behavior predictions.[3] In 1958, Isabel Briggs Myers herself described four distinct personality classifications: probing, scheduling, friendly, and tough-minded.[4] Temperament is an important combination of type preferences that establishes the foundation of one's personality type. Within this foundation lie our needs, values, and talents. Our behaviors tend to organize themselves into patterns upon this foundation.

A PATTERN OF BEHAVIORS

Temperament is best understood as a pattern of consistently observable behaviors. Our temperament is given to us at birth rather than learned, and unless our family of origin provides excess pressure to the contrary, the type preferences that form our temperament will be the primary driving force of our behavior. Even if great external pressures—like our parents or peers—push us to conform to something other than our temperament, we will tend to filter those pressures through our innate temperament.

Temperament determines our development as individuals, for as we grow, who we are becomes more of what we are. Our behaviors cluster into patterns and actions that attempt to satisfy our inner core needs according to personally held values.

Temperament influences everything we do, from what we aspire to, to what we strive zealously to accomplish. And it clearly influences how we manage money. Knowing your own temperament will help you improve your financial habits of spending, giving, borrowing, and saving. If you are married, knowledge of your mate's temperament and a knowledge of how it may complement and conflict with your own will not only enhance your cooperative efforts but also your relationship.

The temperament patterns represent foundational differences in people, but they do not explain all of human behavior. First, each temperament category has observable subcategories that have important differences from each other. Second, such things as developmental issues, family environment, and one's character play major roles in determining behavior. Finally, individuals will adapt to their environment to reduce stress.

As with personality type, the objective is to find out what we are and then to use that understanding to manage our money better. In doing so according to our natural bents, we have the potential to achieve the productivity and inner peace of true wealth. Through temperament, we can recognize and appreciate our strengths as well as identify and work through our weaknesses. Because it is the innate blueprint of the foundation of who we are, temperament is a powerful tool for those motivated to achieve the inner satisfaction that money was designed to provide.

THE ESSENCE OF HUMAN PERSONALITY

If temperament is the foundation of our behavior, then its bricks are communication and the use of tools. According to clinical psychologist and professor David Keirsey, what differentiates us from each other into four distinct dispositions is our use of words and our use of tools. The majority of people are *concrete* (*sensors,* in MBTI terminology) in their use of words, and a minority of people are *abstract* (*intuitives*) in their word usage. About half of us are *cooperative* (*feelers* and *judgers*) in our use of tools, and the other half *pragmatic* (*thinkers* and *perceivers.*)

The language of the Myers-Briggs Type Indicator gives us a way of linking personality preference theory with the four temperaments. The MBTI preference pairs, Extraversion/Introversion, Sensing/Intuition, Thinking/Feeling, and Judging/Perceiving, are used to address our needs, according to the values advanced by each temperament. These preference combinations show themselves in the talents and behaviors that energize us and nurture our inner needs in the most fulfilling way.

While *sensing* and *intuition* describe mental processes, words are the observable output of those processes. Words orient us to the material world by informing ourselves and others what we see, what we think about our vision, and what we believe should be done about it.

Yet, while words define our ends, they do not accomplish them. According to Keirsey, the implementation of goals requires tools, and regardless of what the goals are, each of us will tend to gravitate to one of two categories of tools.

In MBTI terms, feelers and judgers will choose *cooperative tools.* These are tools that have the stamp of approval by the membership groups deemed important by the feelers and judgers. Cooperators strive to achieve their goals by getting along with others, being accommodative and in accord with the established rules, customs and ethos of the social groups they are part of.

Thinkers and perceivers by contrast prefer to focus on finding the best tools for the task at hand, irrespective of any group's approval. The thinkers and perceivers are, therefore, pragmatic in their tool usage. They strive to accomplish their goals in the most efficient way possible, preferably with tools that have the potential to achieve great success with the least possible expenditure of resources. The expectations of the group are of no account to pragmatic tool users unless they become a cost or resource to be considered.

There will, of course, always be situations for concrete word users to communicate abstractly, and for abstract word users to communicate concretely. Likewise, pragmatic tool users can find occasions when they will pursue goals in a cooperative fashion, and sometimes cooperators will go after their ends pragmatically. But our first instinct is always to visualize and describe the world, and then do something about our vision according to our innate temperament patterns.

The combinations of word usage and tool usage derive the four temperament classifications:

Keirsey	Myers-Briggs	Classic Temperament
Concrete-Pragmatist	Sensor-Perceiver (SP)	Sanguine
Abstract-Pragmatist	Intuitive-Thinker (NT)	Phlegmatic
Concrete-Cooperator	Sensor-Judger (SJ)	Melancholic
Abstract-Cooperator	Intuitive-Feeler (NF)	Choleric

Given that money "talks" in a universally understood language and that it is the most commonly used tool in everyday life, the applicability of the temperament model of word and tool usage cannot be understated. An understanding of our temperament is essential to an understanding of our money personality. With that in mind, complete exercise 8 and see if it confirms the temperament pattern you found in exercise 7.

Exercise 8

KEY ELEMENTS OF THE TEMPERAMENTS

As a start to verifying your temperament pattern, read through the brief descriptions of the basic elements of each of the four temperaments below.

SJ
Skilled in *logistics*
Responsible, dutiful, concerned

Life quest: *belonging*
Achilles' Heel: *disarray/ disorganization*

SP
Skilled in *tactics*
Spontaneous, flexible, and resourceful in meeting challenges
Life quest: *action*
Achilles' Heel: *routine*

NF
Skilled in *diplomacy*
Central focus in life is *relationships*

Life quest: *identity*
Achilles' Heel: *guilt*

NT
Skilled in *strategy*
Driven to *understand* events by logical, impersonal analysis
Life quest: *competency*
Achilles' Heel: *incompetence,* first in self, then in others

Now continue on your path to discovering your money personality by studying the in-depth temperament descriptions below.

THE FOUR TEMPERAMENTS REVISITED

As we noted in the beginning of this chapter, for 2,500 years observers have given different names to each of the four temperaments. I have chosen labels that I feel best epitomize the values and actions that each temperament typically manifests their behaviors with money: *protectors, players, pleasers,* and *planners.* The following is an overview of each temperament. You will have aspects of each, but one of the four will suit you the best.

99

The Protector

Protectors have a natural disposition to observe and preserve resulting from their integration of a preference for sensing (focus on facts and details, with an orientation to the present moment) and a preference for judging (pursuit of closure, structure, and organization). To protectors, *life is a process* of cultivating the good life, which to them means being comfortable and secure by organizing and preserving their present environment. They are motivated by *stability, security, community, family,* and *virtue.* Protectors are life's guardians, trustees, and administrators.

Of the four temperaments, the protector is the *most responsible.* It's not that responsibility is not important to the other three, it's just that the protector lives to show herself as dutiful. Like Dorothy, her quest is to find a place where she belongs, a group in which she can be a significant member by serving it. The most important membership to have is family, nuclear and extended, but the goal is to make every group she is part of feel like a family.

Once she finds her place in personally meaningful associations, a protector feels it is her duty to make sure all the needs of the group are consistently met. This she will try to do by creating procedures and structure to preserve and protect the group. Protectors are the backbone of their organizations.

Protectors have *a gift of administration,* making sure that whatever needs to get done, does get done. They work long and hard, are prompt, painstakingly thorough, and utterly dependable. When protectors say they will do something, they *will* do it, no matter what it takes. Their word is their bond because their need to belong is fulfilled by the satisfaction of oral contracts between themselves and others. They have a low regard for people who do not do as they say.

Their natural giftings guide protectors to *activities that produce structure, morality, security, and respectability,* so that life can be maintained in a simplified and orderly fashion. They aspire to be good and faithful stewards, to doing the right thing, being actively involved in operations, and making sure others are happy with the service provided.

Protectors *value being concerned.* Because they care so much, protectors take life seriously. They are conservative by nature, placing great faith in the experiences of the past and fretting about the unknowns of the future, which could disrupt what they've worked so hard to govern and regulate. As such, the protectors' *trademark line* is, "If it ain't broke, don't fix it." Change is hard for protectors to embrace, especially when it threatens long-standing traditions. Protectors make change slowly, by evolution rather than revolution, to see if change is working and therefore worth continuing. A sense of heritage and "where I came from" is critical to the protectors' identity, and they will fight to maintain significant links to their past.

Protectors are at their best when they are allowed by their authority figures to take responsibility to provide order and organization. They will flourish in an environment of gratitude and demonstrate a remarkable capability for administration; dependability; the ability to take charge and always knowing who's in charge.[5]

All the temperament types benefit by the preservation of past wisdom and the stabilizing role that the protector's provide to the world. Possible examples of protectors include Moses, George Washington, Mother Teresa, Norman Rockwell, and Colin Powell.[6]

The Player

Players have a natural disposition to observe and react, resulting from their integration of a preference for sensing (focus on facts and details, with an orientation to the present moment) and a preference for perceiving (pursuit of spontaneity, flexibility, and adaptability). To the player, *life is a process* of doing whatever feels good at the moment, trusting their impulses and seeking to make an impression at whatever they're doing. They are motivated by *liberation from emotional or social inhibitions and the need for intensity of experience.* Players are life's artisans, participators, and the life of every party.

Of the four temperaments, the player is the *most free spirited.* While each of the four temperaments yearns to be free to do a particular thing, the player's craving is to be free from restraint to do anything—whatever the moment demands. Like the Lion, his quest is to find opportunities to experience and enjoy life through the display of nerve and bravado. For the player, the most important thing is to "Just do it!" as the popular commercial exhorts. In response to doing "it," the protector would ask what, where, and when; the pleaser (as we will see) would want to know with who or for who; and the planner (as we will also see) would ask, "Why?" But to the player, such reasoning would be irrelevant and rob them of the sheer joy of doing something for no other reason than they simply can, therefore, they must!

Players have *a gift of being highly attuned to whatever is happening now* and of the ability to adapt themselves to the needs of the moment for maximum impact and effect. In contrast to protectors who try to fit each situation into their experience, players enjoy situations that give them new experiences. As such, they are great responders to crisis and in dealing with unpredictability. But they shine in good times, too. Easily caught up in the moment, the player has a *joie de vivre* that is more intense than any other temperament.

Their natural giftings guide players to *activities that have immediate outcomes and high impact.* They relish a sense of danger and therefore will "push the envelope," seeking to explore and conquer uncharted territories, whether they be emotional, physical, spiritual—and financial! They aspire to display their virtuosity and bravado by doing that which hasn't been done before, to accomplish the previously unimaginable.

Players *value excitement.* They are by nature incurable optimists, always believing that the next roll of the dice is the one that will pay off. I used to say about Steve, still the most outrageous player I know, that he'd risk it all on one-in-a-million odds because he just *knew* that the *one* was him! Since taking risks is what makes players feel most alive, they are prone to live through series of reversals of fortune, going from victor to vanquished, yet always eager to try again. As such, players have many trademark lines, including "Easy come, easy go," and "Strike while the iron is hot!" Players live in the here and now.

Players are at their best in an open atmosphere or surroundings that provide competition, opportunity, and the freedom to trust their impulses rather than the system. They will flourish in an environment of stimulation, variety, and freedom, and of appreciation by others for their flair and sense of adventure. Players have a remarkable capability for practicality; adept problem-solving skills, particularly at hands-on tasks; resourcefulness; and a special sense of immediate needs.[7]

All the temperament types benefit by the "can-do" responsiveness to crisis, the rejection of outdated or unnecessary constraints, and the uninhibited zest for life that the players provide to the world. Possible examples of players include King David, George Patton, Amelia Earhart, Elvis Presley, and Michael Jordan.

The Pleaser

Pleasers have *a natural disposition* to focus on possibilities for people from their integration of a preference for intuition (focus on patterns and meanings, with an orientation to future possibilities) and a preference for feeling (deciding by empathetically striving for harmony and positive interactions). To the pleaser, *life is a process* of cultivating relationships, personal growth, and making the world a better place by helping others reach their potential. They are motivated by *growth in consciousness achieved through reflective self-renewal and growth in wellness*—physical, emotional, and spiritual. Pleasers are life's idealistic humanitarians, encouragers, mentors, and counselors.

Of the four temperaments, the pleaser is the *most empathetic.* It's not that empathy is not important to the other three, it's just that the pleaser lives to be connected to the feelings of others. Like the Tin Man, the pleaser's quest is to seek his identity and meaning through nurturing and meaningful relationships. The most important relationships are those that are deeply personal and mutually edifying, and with a spirit of cooperation and teamwork.

Pleasers have *a gift of seeing the potential and capabilities that others don't see* in themselves. They seemingly have x-ray vision into the soul, discerning people's unspoken issues and feelings and then articulating deep truths, often in the form of encouragement, about those feelings.

Their natural giftings guide pleasers to *activities that are meaningful* rather than necessary (protectors), entertaining (players), or visionary (planners, as we will see). They are drawn to pursuits that promote human interests, especially those where they can transmit ideas through words, such as teaching, humanities, counseling, and religion. They aspire to be the best they can be as the way of doing the best thing for others.

Pleasers *value being "real" and take having personal integrity very seriously.* They are warm and nurturing by nature, and find themselves energized by the untapped potential that lies within whoever they come into contact with. As such, the pleasers' trademark line is, "Be all that you can be." However, their enthusiasm for people can be frustrated if they sense an unwillingness or unreadiness to grow, or detect the presence of unethical beliefs.

Pleasers are at their best when they can see themselves helping others in insightful ways. They will flourish in nurturing environments that emphasize personal interaction, teamwork, and receptivity to creative ideas. Where this is the case, pleasers will demonstrate a remarkable capability for working with people and drawing out their best; being articulate and persuasive; a strong desire to help others; and the ability to affirm others freely and easily.[8]

All the temperament types benefit by the role of conduit for new, spiritually oriented influences, often expressed in a utopian humanitarianism, that the pleasers provide to the world. Possible examples of pleasers include Joan of Arc, Ghandi, Martin Luther King, Jr., and Emily Dickinson.

The Planner

Planners have a natural disposition to focus on possibilities and concepts for systems from their integration of a preference for intuition (focus on patterns and meanings, with an orientation to future possibilities) and a preference for thinking (deciding by striving for objective and logical standards of truth). To the planner, *life is a process of acquiring expertise, relentlessly pursuing excellence,* and wherever and whenever possible, *challenging conventional thought.* They are motivated by *ambition* and *achievement.* Planners are life's visionaries, innovators, and strategists.

Of the four temperaments, the planner is the most independent. He prefers to direct himself according to his own high standards. Like the Scarecrow, his quest is more knowledge, more learning, more questions, and more intellectual progress. The most important thing is to be knowledgeable, knowing why things are and why they work as they do—and then making them better.

Planners have *a gift of seeing with their "mind's eye" the unformed future and creating a strategy for making it a reality.* They can move easily from abstract possibilities down to the details and parameters. They are the human computers that easily analyze, synthesize, and prioritize large amounts of information.

Their natural giftings guide planners to *activities that involve learning and acquiring skills.* To the planner, work is play and it's especially enjoyable if it leads to new levels of expertise. Planners also enjoy competition, first with themselves and then with others, as a way of rating themselves. They aspire to wizardry, to be able to predict and control the outcome of events through their absolute knowledge and understanding of the principles and principals involved.

Planners *value achievement, competence, and purity of thought and expression.* They are intellectually curious problem solvers by nature, and they will find a problem even if one doesn't exist! A planner's trademark line is, "There's more than one way to skin a cat." It had to be a planner that invented the terms "better mousetrap" and "paradigm shift."

Planners are at their best at innovative and intellectually stimulating projects where they are widely regarded as "the best person for the job." They will thrive in idea-centered environments that are critical, competitive, and creative. Where this is the case, planners will demonstrate a remarkable capability for readily seeing the big picture; conceptualizing and planning systems; discerning the internal logic and underlying principles of systems and organizations; and the ability to speak and write clearly and precisely.[9]

All the temperament types benefit by the planners taking new ideas and making them real, and their passion for excellence. Possible examples of planners include King Solomon, Thomas Jefferson, Madame Curie, Walt Disney, and Bill Gates.

Temperaments Yesterday and Today

Far from being the dry categories created by ivory-tower researchers, the four temperaments help us understand ourselves and others. They also give us a zeal and focus in life. Stephen Covey, author of *The Seven Habits of Highly Effective People,* noted that within the nature of man are four fundamental endowments. These qualities separate people from even the most intelligent of animals. What are they? [10]

- Self-awareness. That's the ability to think about one's own thought process.
- Imagination. That's the ability to create in our minds beyond our present reality.
- Conscience. This quality gives every man and woman a deep inner awareness of right and wrong.
- Independent will. People are able to act based upon their self-awareness, free from all other influences.

Significantly, in describing these four fundamental aspects of human nature, Covey has spotlighted four driving forces behind each of the four classic temperaments:

- self-awareness, a driving force of the *pleaser* (NF)
- imagination, a driving force of the *planner* (NT)
- conscience, a driving force of the *protector* (SJ)
- independent will, a driving force of the *player* (SP)

These four temperaments will influence the perspectives and therefore writings of historians. For instance, in the New Testament gospel accounts, the same basic story is told from four different points of view, each influenced by the personalities of the authors. It is utterly fascinating that the four gospel writers faithfully conform to the classic temperaments observed through the ages.

- Matthew is the protector's gospel. Matthew was a tax collector, a profession that would attract many SJ temperaments. Fitting for a protector, Matthew's focus was on the preservation of the Jewish heritage. Matthew showed his love of the past by beginning with a genealogy and his love of duty by ending with the Great Commission, which is what he felt is the responsibility of all of Jesus' followers.

- Mark is the player's gospel. Mark recorded the life of Christ as seen through the eyes of Simon Peter, Jesus' impulsive disciple. Mark provided no real beginning or ending to his fast-paced narrative. Instead he focused on what Jesus did and Jesus' joyful freedom in making an impact on others. Consistent with Peter's SP temperament, Mark recorded more miracles than any gospel writer despite writing the shortest of the four accounts.

- Luke is the pleaser's gospel. Luke was a doctor, a profession common to many NF temperaments. Luke was writing to his friend about the life-changing possibilities of Jesus' teachings. Luke's gospel has the most stories about people and how the wisdom of Christ's teachings changed their lives for the better.

- John is the planner's gospel. Planners are usually talented wordsmiths, so it is natural that John saw Christ as the Word, the ultimate expression of written thought, a very figurative concept that would come easily to an abstract word user. In keeping with his NT temperament, John's purpose for writing was to provide a systematic and logical argument for the validity of Christ's claims of divinity.

Whether it's how we write a history, relate with our spouse, or prefer to use money, our inborn temperament pattern has important implications. Your temperament and your Myers-Briggs personality type will influence your financial thoughts and actions as each of the personality type preferences has differing impacts on how people handle money and finances. The next chapter will take an in-depth look at the implications of personality preferences on your financial actions.

PART THREE

Mind Over Money

CHAPTER SEVEN

Your Financial Behavior

> A wise man should have money in his head,
> not in his heart.
>
> — *Jonathan Swift*

While shopping with my daughter a couple of years ago, I saw the following graduation cards that had temperament undertones:

The first card featured an eager beaver (whose favorite subjects were probably gym, lunch, and recess) joyously dancing atop a messy stack of books and school supplies, arms spread to the heavens, flashing a toothy grin and mouth open wide, relishing the end of school, as if to say, "Free at last! I'm free at last!" This was the player (sensor perceiver) in action.

The second card pictured a traditional cap sitting atop three neatly stacked books; a scroll bound with a ribbon sits next to the books. Some flowers are in the background. This was the protector (sensor judger).

The third card showed scientist Albert Einstein. His classic formula, $E = mc^2$, was written below him, and the word *Knowledge* was written in bold above. This depicted the planner (intuitive thinker).

The fourth card showed a boy carrying packed bags, putting a heart into a large box marked "Life," leaving home to go out onto a road leading to the big world beyond. The card was entitled, "Put Your Heart into It." That captured well the essence of the pleaser (intuitive feeler).

Those cards summarize the different values and behavior of the four temperaments we have discussed. Clearly those values will also affect our financial behavior, including our purchases. Imagine yourself buying a new car. You're at the car lot and spot the car of your dreams. What is the first thing that comes to mind? Or imagine you're at the furniture store looking at new bedroom furniture. You see the perfect bedroom set. Again, what might be your first thoughts?

Now take these two imaginary scenarios back one step. What led you into the market for a new car or bedroom furnishings in the first place?

In chapter 1 we learned about utiles, an unconscious measure of satisfaction of the value that we assign to things or activities. Recall that if something is very satisfying to us, it can be said that it provides us with a lot of utiles. The reason utiles are so important is that they motivate us to self-expression through our use of money.

But satisfaction of utiles requires us to match finite resources to limitless prospective ways to use these resources. Not only do we have to recognize our utiles, but when, where, and how to use our money to satisfy them. Every use of money, or contemplated use of money, whether making a purchase, window shopping, or just daydreaming, is a problem to solve.

Good problem solving involves the sequential use of four personality processes—*sensing, intuition, thinking,* and *feeling.* Sensing identifies the current facts, and intuition sees the future possibilities given the facts. Thinking then analyzes all the information to decide the logical consequences of acting on each alternative, considering the pros and cons and determining the costs and benefits. Finally, feeling weighs how much we care about each of the possibilities, striving to preserve harmony by taking into account people's feelings, interests, and values.

Although this is a straightforward process, it is difficult to implement because most people tend to rely on only those processes that are the easiest for them to use, and ignore those that they are least comfortable with. Starting in childhood, they tended to rely on one preference more than the others because it seemed more natural to them. The more they used it, the more mature and skilled this process became. Eventually they came to make most of their decisions—especially important ones—according to the characteristics of this favored mental process.

Thus, one of these four preferences of sensing, intuition, thinking or feeling, has come to command our thought processes, regardless of our personality type. Because this chosen preference draws more attention and energy than the other three, it becomes the focal point of our personality type. It is called our "dominant process" because it commands our personality. Even if the decision is the best one under the circumstances, we will find it difficult to be sure of any decision that is arrived at without significant input from our dominant process. *Perhaps the biggest reason for money not buying happiness is that it is spent contrary to your preferred decision-making process.*

FOUR WAYS OF SPENDING MONEY

Each personality type will approach problem solving differently, and therefore the person has his or her own reasons for their particular approach to money management. Your own personality type is one of sixteen possible types. Each of the sixteen types makes primary use of either the sensing, intuition, thinking, or feeling function to make psychologically satisfying financial decisions.

Of the sixteen personality types, four are dominant sensors, four are dominant intuitives, four are dominant thinkers, and four are dominant feelers. First, look at the characteristics of your own group, then compare your focus to that of the other three groups. This will not only affirm your style of financial decision making, but confirm your suspicion that not everybody approaches money the same way that you do.

You could say that your dominant preference is automatically tuned into your utiles, and so it is the first one that comes to mind when it comes to thinking about money.

For example, when Jeff and Carol went shopping for a car, they brought different points of view to bear on the decision. Jeff's view was from a "big picture" perspective, focused on their overall financial condition, how the car would fit in terms of their lifestyle for the next few years, and various alternatives: new or used, lease or buy, competing brands and competing dealerships. Carol's point of view was from a relational perspective. Her focus was on safety, practicality for family trips, viability in winter, and the capability to carry a load of children. The "alternatives" she presented to Jeff were pretty simple: "Buy the car I want or else!"

Through my financial counseling and my own studies of financial behaviors, I have come to believe that the most important personality-related determinant of financial actions is a person's dominant preference. In terms of your own approach to money, more of the differences between you and other people can be explained by your dominant preference than any other aspect of personality type.

Dominant Sensors: "The time is now!"

Although the overall personalities of each of the four dominant sensors are quite different they share a great deal in common. Dominant sensors (ISTJ, ISFJ, ESTP, ESFP) see money as a source of funds to achieve tangible, practical, near-term results. They are likely to:

- have a heightened awareness and clear understanding of present physical needs especially regarding food, clothing, shelter, and supplies;
- excel at attending to facts and figures, such as price, quantity, and availability;
- be confident when making financial decisions that rely on firsthand prior experience or tradition;
- sacrifice future enjoyment or gain, orienting their finances to achieve near-term, practical, tangible results; and
- not spend much time designing solutions or generating alternatives to analyze.

Other sensors (ISTP, ISFP, ESTJ, ESFJ) share these traits but not to the degree of dominant sensors. According to veteran type watchers Otto Kroeger and Janet Theusen, sensors are at their best when they have reliable facts and evidence to work with. They are most adept at solving problems that they can get their arms around and then purposefully move toward immediate, practical, and visible results. They are very sensitive about wasting time and therefore can be very impatient with theorizing or brainstorming about problems that are not immediately critical.

Dominant Intuitives: "Building a better tomorrow."

Although the overall personalities of each of the four dominant intuitives are quite different, they share a great deal in common. Dominant intuitives (INTJ, INFJ, ENTP, ENFP) see money as a resource that provides for future possibilities and to meet tomorrow's goals. They are likely to:

- excel at seeing connections and possibilities that are unseen by others, and be indifferent to what others do with their money;
- be mindful about the big picture, seeing with their "mind's eye" the long-term implications of today's financial actions;
- be imaginative with their finances, frequently employing complex strategies to accomplish their financial goals;
- be confident about making decisions after all the alternatives have been considered that cover every conceivable aspect of a situation; and
- sacrifice present enjoyment, preferring to orient their finances around having enough money available to be able to satisfy whatever possibilities may inspire them in the future.

Other intuitives (INTP, INFP, ENTJ, ENFJ) share these traits but not to the degree of dominant intuitives. For intuitives, problems are best solved when they are set in a big picture context. A household budget is merely part of a larger financial planning issue that has tax, investment, insurance, and net worth implications, issues about which information must be gathered in order to have an effective household budget.

Dominant Thinkers: "Use your head!"

Although the overall personalities of each of the four dominant thinkers are quite different, they share a great deal in common. Usually, money matters most to dominant thinkers (INTP, ISTP, ENTJ, ESTJ), who see money as a pragmatic tool to achieve power, control and measurable success. They are likely to:

- excel at analyzing facts and figures;
- be mindful about "what the data says";
- have objective standards for what makes a "good" financial decision: staying within budget, achieving a target return on investment, minimizing taxes and debt;
- be confident about making decisions after impersonally analyzing the potential consequences of any given financial action: pros and cons, plusses and minuses, costs and benefits, causes and effects; and
- be critical evaluators of their own financial achievements and skeptical of advice from others.

Other thinkers (INTJ, ISTJ, ENTP, ESTP) share these traits but not to the degree of dominant thinkers. Thinkers have a natural awareness of the possible consequences of financial decisions. Although thinkers may have strong emotions about an issue, they don't find them reliable as decision-making input, preferring instead to trust analysis of the data.

Dominant Feelers: "You gotta have heart."

Although the overall personalities of each of the four dominant feelers are quite different, they share a great deal in common. Money often doesn't matter much to dominant feelers (ISFP, INFP, ESFJ, ENFJ), who see money as a source of funds to support what is valued to themselves and others. They are likely to:

- excel at evaluating situations in human terms;
- be mindful of what "their heart says", using their emotions as a barometer for the interpersonal consequences of any financial action;
- have case-by-case standards for what makes a good financial decision;

- be confident about making decisions only after weighing how those who might be impacted by a financial decision will feel; and

- be supportive of using money in ways that promote harmony or improve others' lives, especially immediate family.

Other feelers (ISFJ, INFJ, ESFP, ENFP) share these traits but not to the degree of dominant feelers. Feelers have a radar system tuned into how other people will react to problems and their resolutions. In problem solving, their focus are the relational issues, and they turn to their emotions for guidance on how to proceed.

The four dominant preferences as well as the four temperaments we looked at in chapter 6 clearly affect our financial behavior, and your personality type and temperament may influence your financial thoughts and actions. Each of the sixteen sets of MBTI preferences has differing impacts on how people handle money and finances. Therefore, your natural style of approaching life has implications for your everyday financial actions, especially as it pertains to four factors: needs, values, talents, and behaviors.

In general, we can define behavior with the following formula:

Behavior = how we use our talents, according to our values, to satisfy our needs

To make the most of your money personality, you must: (1) identify your needs; (2) clarify your values; (3) affirm your talents; and (4) understand your behavior, which occurs when you complete the first three tasks. Let's look at how we can recognize our needs and values and how to affirm our talents.

NEEDS

Because meeting our needs is what we require for physiological and psychological well-being, true wealth begins here. Without identifying and affirming what our needs are, and then adapting our values and talents to meet them, we run the risk of becoming skilled at things that are meaningless. Ultimately, if money is to matter, we must use it to achieve that which we are yearning for and seeking after the most.

When needs are met, we are energized and satisfied. When they are unmet, we are drained of energy and experience dissatisfaction and stress. The discomfort of unmet needs may drive us to cope in unhealthy and ineffective ways. Clarification of our needs helps us to be aware of what motivates us and provides us with clues as to what may bring us the most long-term satisfaction.

Recall from chapter 5 that each of us has a primary life quest that emanates from our temperament, our individual pattern of interrelated characteristics. In chapter 1, we considered how our uses of money tend to be dominated by needs arising out of one of four domains: physical, mental, emotional, and social. These domains and their associated needs are influenced by your personality type, in particular, your temperament and dominant preference.

Table 1

TEMPERAMENT AND ONE'S AREA OF NEED

Temperament	Domain that needs are met in
Protectors (SJ), especially ESTJ	Physical—relating to the body, material things or our physical surrounding
Planners (NT), especially ENTP, INTJ	Mental—relating to the mind and intellect
Pleasers (NF), especially INFP, ENFJ	Emotional—relating to subjective feelings or sensibilities in regards to yourself or important interpersonal relationship
Players (SP), especially ESTP, ESFP	Social—relating to family, friendly relations or companionship, or occupied with matters affecting human welfare (including business)

The preceding table shows the relationship between temperament and financially related areas of need. At this point you have identified your temperament and you should spot the domain in which your needs are dominant.

Another dimension affecting what we see as our primary needs is our motivation, the emotions and desires that operate on our wills and stimulate us to act. While motivation can come from external sources such as inducements, incentives, or coercion, generally it arises as a natural expression of our innate personality. Our motivation is a psychological force that compels us to act to assure that our needs are met.

As we also saw in chapter 1, there are six common motives for financial actions, and under motivation (page 27), you were asked to rank your top three motives in your financial decisions. In terms of what motivates people financially, there is a great deal of similarity as to how people rank these six motivations. My studies indicate that the following is the most common ranking of financial motives:

1. comfort and convenience
2. security and protection
3. emotional satisfaction
4. avoidance of loss
5. financial gain
6. pride

While these rankings are fairly consistent across the personality preferences, personality type still plays a role in determining financial motives. For example, although planners (NT temperament) rank financial gain and pride among their lesser motives, just as do the other temperaments, planners will be influenced by these motives slightly more than the other temperaments. This stands to reason because planners, especially ENTP's and INTJ's (dominant intuitives) are future oriented and competency driven.

Likewise, other manifestations of personality type have slight natural biases for or against each financial motivation. The following table summarizes these tendencies:

Table 2

MOTIVATION CLASHES

Motive	Bias for	Bias against
Comfort and convenience	All players (SP), ENTJ, ESTJ	All planners (NT)
Security and protection	ISTJ, ISFJ	ESTP, ESFP
Emotional satisfaction	INFP, ENFJ	ENTJ, ESTJ
Avoidance of loss	All introverts	All extraverts
Financial gain	All planners (NT), especially ENTP, INTJ	ESFP, ESTP
Pride	All planners (NT), especially ENTP, INTJ	All pleasers (NF)

Of course, conflict and misunderstanding can arise when two individuals of differing personality types bring different motives to the table. For instance, food is a physical need, yet where to eat it is a function of financial motivation. Pleasers (NF temperaments) seek the emotional satisfaction that comes from the aesthetics, ambience, and atmosphere of fine restaurants. That's a real problem if they want to go out to eat with an ISTJ or ESTJ, who typically look for the comfort and convenience of an all-you-can-eat buffet for $3.95 as close to home as possible.

VALUES, TALENTS, BEHAVIORS

Values are the deep-rooted beliefs we have about what is good, desirable, and innately worthwhile. Values are what is important to us. They define our character, supply meaning to our work and play, and influence our decisions. Values are the enduring characteristics or aspects of life that we consider vital to our satisfaction.

Throughout life you will make choices based upon your values, and values frequently come into play when you have to decide how to use your money. Values are personal, and sometimes personality driven, and a frequent source of interpersonal conflict is the incorrect assumption that others share our values. Therefore, clarifying our values will help us to determine ways in which money enriches us beyond the merely financial aspects.

Table 3

"VALUES CLASHES"

Personality-driven values differences that have financial implications include:

Value	High Priority	Low Priority
To have people like me To do things for my family and others	Dominant Feelers: ISFP, INFP, ESFJ, ENFJ	Dominant Thinkers: INTP, ISTP, ENTJ, ESTJ
To be able to do things I want to do To do what is right according to my beliefs	Dominant Thinkers: INTP, ISTP, ENTJ, ESTJ	Dominant Feelers: ISFP, INFP, ESFJ, ENFJ
To be able to do things well	Dominant Intuitives: INTJ, INFJ, ENTP, ENFP	Dominant Sensors: ISFJ, ISTJ, ESTP, ESFP
To do new and different things often	Perceiving types	Judging types
To have as many of the good things of life as I can	Judging types	Perceiving types

Again, conflict can occur when two individuals have different values. Table 3 shows the differences in personality-driven values that have financial implications. Where are you in these values, according to the table? If someone else is assisting in the financial decisions, does he or she have a conflicting value? Remember, values may not always represent truth; they represent what is important to us.

Talents

Talents are natural gifts and abilities that require little energy output. This results in high performance and increased self-esteem. Because these skills come easy to us they are not always known. Affirmation of our talents helps us to identify our natural abilities and what types of roles will capitalize on them. Using our talents may reduce stress and provide the greatest opportunity for satisfaction. The greatest financial impact of our talents will usually be felt in our career choices.

Behaviors

Behaviors are the result of our attempts to satisfy our needs. They are the everyday actions that can be observed or demonstrated. Understanding our behaviors can help us appreciate why we do what we do, and what things we can do to bring us the greatest satisfaction of our needs.

TEMPERAMENT AND MONEY

Let's return to the four primary temperaments and see how they affect our money decisions. Here is a summary of the four primary temperaments, focusing on their implications for our financial decisions.

Protectors (SJ): Most Responsible

For protectors, *the good life* is preserving a comfortable, secure, and organized home and work environment. Their *behaviors* show protectors to be economical, structured, conservative, and cautious, with an orientation on the past.

The talents of the four personality types labeled as protectors are:

- ISTJ—being dependable and responsible administrators, especially for the day-to-day organization and record keeping necessary to keeping things running "shipshape"

- ISFJ—offering sensible and practical attention to the daily needs of others, creating procedures to provide stability and efficiency
- ESTJ—efficiently managing resources according to goals and plans to meet day-to-day concerns
- ESFJ—hospitality, knowing what matters to others, and then organizing and administering groups to serve other groups

Protectors naturally handle money conservatively and purposefully in order to provide themselves with a solid financial foundation. As the spouse of one protector said, "My husband is truly concerned with financial security for now and the future. He's a terrific provider and is secure with who he is and what he does. I feel fortunate to have a spouse who is so seriously focused on financial security." The weakness of protectors is that they can be overwhelmed by disorganization, vague situations, or unanticipated change. Sloppy record keeping, unbalanced checkbooks, and being unable to do what needs to be done is very stressful for protectors.

Players (SP): Most Free-Spirited

For players, *the good life* is having the freedom to do what feels good and make an impression. Their *behaviors* show players to be spontaneous, impulsive, risk-taking, and present-oriented.

The talents of the four personality types labeled as players are:

- ESTP—finding the most expedient way to do or fix something *right now,* especially as it relates to hands-on physical property
- ESFP—being generous and bringing enjoyment to themselves and others through tangible acts of service or planning community events
- ISTP—finding the best, most pragmatic way to handle necessary tasks (such as maintenance and repairs)
- ISFP—altruistic, giving immediate, direct support to others needs

Players are naturally bold and opportunistic, inclined to bear the risks associated with special situations that may improve their financial situation. As one player put it, "Anything I want I just put on the charge account. Years ago I did overextend. I'm more the take-a-chance personality. What have you got to lose—it's only money! Life is to be enjoyed." The weaknesses of players are that they are not goal oriented and may have too great a penchant for financial risk. Being forced to stay within limits is stressful for players; that's why they're inclined to borrow when funds are limited.

Pleasers (NF): Most Empathetic

For pleasers, *the good life* is cultivating relationships, growing personally, and helping others achieve their potential. Their *behaviors* show pleasers to be focused on relationships and personal involvement, with an orientation on the future.

The talents of the four personality types labeled as pleasers are:

- ENFP—sharing resources and building relationships
- ENFJ—large-scale organizing of activities that promote long-lasting fellowship and harmony
- INFP—providing a positive vision for the future, especially as it relates to human potential
- INFJ—creating an atmosphere of mutual trust where they can lead others to develop and grow in insightful ways

Pleasers are naturally altruistic, willing to devote substantial portions of their financial wealth to the betterment of others. The weakness of pleasers is their general apathy about money, which can result in a weak present financial foundation and poor preparation for the future. However, one thing pleasers care deeply about is quality and aesthetics, and settling for less than their ideal can be difficult for them. Also, not being able to meet the needs of others, especially family, and interpersonal conflict over money is very stressful for pleasers. Pleasers are the most idealistic of all temperaments, and it shows in their shopping habits. They find themselves looking at the highest quality and most expensive merchandise, and while they are particularly pleased to buy the best at a reduced price, they are also content to do without before settling for lower quality.

Planners (NT): Most Independent

For planners, *the good life* is challenging one's self to acquire expertise and pursue excellence. Their *behaviors* show planners to be problem solving, pursuing excellence, and skeptical, with a future/infinite orientation.

The talents of the four personality types labeled as planners are:

- ENTP—resourcefulness, particularly in developing imaginative financial strategies, and challenging personal or organizational achievement
- ENTJ—executing long-range plans: development, organization, mobilization, and implementation
- INTP—providing an orderly approach to financial issues, and insight into the long-term consequences of any given course of action
- INTJ—long-range planning and finding new approaches, envisioning ways to create a better quality of life

Planners naturally develop strategic plans to ensure a comfortable financial future. Their weakness is that these plans may be overly complex resulting in "paralysis of analysis" and very little accomplished. Planners feel stress when they cannot see adequate progress toward future financial goals, and being forced to stick to the "tried and true," when they have in mind "new and improved." Planners, especially extraverts (ENTP, ENTJ) can be very competitive and see financial transactions like house or car buying as a game to win. This intensity can be disconcerting for spouses of planners.

A classic example of the money personality differences due to temperament can be seen with the motives behind buying luxury automobiles. All four temperaments will buy luxury cars, but for different reasons, as table 4 shows.

Table 4
WHO BUYS LUXURY CARS?

Protectors (SJ):	for the quality, tradition, safety, and long-lasting investment value
Players (SP):	for the unadulterated and unrestrained pleasure of driving it, whether or not it makes sense financially
Pleasers (NF):	for the ambience (as long as its not too opulent), the uniqueness, and the comfort it would provide for their friends
Planners (NT):	to manifest their highly refined tastes and their acumen in accumulating enough money to buy one

JUDGING VS. PERCEIVING: HOW WE INTERACT WITH THE EXTERNAL WORLD

The last letter of your four-letter type is a third critical de-terminant of your money personality. It reflects which func-tion—information gathering (perceiving) or decision making (judging)—you prefer to use in the external world. Because money is a tool that is used in the external world, we will find that our lifestyle is greatly influenced by our preference for judging or perceiving.

If you are a judger, you prefer your finances to be managed in a planned and orderly way, seeking to use money as a tool to regulate and direct life. You see financial activities as deci-sions to make, close, and move on. For judgers, planning their work and working their plan is how they get things done in a satisfactory and stress free manner.

If you are a perceiver, you prefer your finances to be man-aged in a way that allows flexibility and spontaneity. Detailed plans and final decisions feel confining, as you prefer to stay open to new possibilities and last-minute options—even after the last minute is up! Rather than plan their work, perceivers go with the flow, preferring to plan for serendipity.

Left to its own devices, the perceiver's serendipity may occasionally result in financial success. However, it is typically the judgers who achieve better financial results. After all, financial management is ultimately a decision-making process, one that usually better fits the judger's natural self-disciplined, "no muss, no fuss" style. Because many perceivers regard *plan* as a four-letter curse word, it is quite common that, compared to judgers, perceivers will: (1) spend money today, as if there is no tomorrow; (2) "max out" credit cards more often; and (3) feel "out of control" with their finances.

Besides the fact that judgers like budgets and perceivers don't, and that judgers pay bills early and perceivers don't see the big deal about being a few days late, the classic difference between them is seen at income tax time. Before the ink is dry on their W-2, judgers have filed their returns and begin waiting impatiently for their refunds—which they're getting because they actually took the time to plan their deductions. Meanwhile, perceivers typically are lined up at the post office on April 15, waiting to get their 11:59 P.M. postmark—on their request for a four month extension!

HOW DO YOU LIKE TO BUY?

Susan Brock, consulting psychologist and principal of Brock Associates, has identified four different kinds of customers based upon their personality type. Her work has found that clear patterns of buying behavior emerge when you consider the two middle letters of the four-letter MBTI type: ST, SF, NF, NT.[1] Although there will be differences within the four groups based upon the critical judger-perceiver dichotomy and less critical extravert-introvert dichotomy, in general Brock found that:

- ST customers buy the facts, specific features, logically presented, with a focus on responsibly meeting practical needs.

- SF customers buy personalized service, forming a bond of loyalty to the brand, vendor, person or product that gives them personal and individualized service.

- NF customers buy a concept, in the form of products that support their vision of what can be, especially as it relates to other people.
- NT customers buy options, looking for products that make sense from a long-range perspective, that can adjust to fit changing circumstances or future needs.

T (thinkers) buyers, whether ST or NT, focus on the objective merits of a prospective purchase relative to their own needs and are not typically concerned what other people think. F (feelers) buyers, whether SF or NF, focus on the interpersonal merits of a purchase, and what others think and need is valuable input to their buying process. One NF woman said, "When out shopping I hesitate to spend money on myself, whereas my husband is always saying, 'Get what you want.'"

The introvert-extravert and judger-perceiver dichotomies modify the themes common to these four buying patterns. Extraverted customers like to "talk it out," going out shopping with others and asking salespeople lots of questions. Introverts like to "think it through." They prefer to shop alone or with one other person they're close to, making catalogs and the Internet their favorite modes of shopping. As you might imagine, malls are extravert territory (and the bane of an introvert's existence), while small, off-the-beaten-track specialty shops are the province of introverts. Introverts tend not to engage salespeople in conversation, preferring to listen patiently and take home written material to study and think about it.

Judging and perceiving also affect the buying process. The judgers' "joy of closure" impels them to a short sales process: "See target, hit target, move on to next target." For perceivers, who take pleasure in the "joy of processing," the shopping experience is often more fun than the actual purchase, which is often described as being anticlimactic. As opposed to hitting the target, perceivers want to question whether it's the right target, consider many other alternative targets, and know as much as possible about each target. When perceivers are unable to decide on one choice, they may "decide" on more than one, even if that's not affordable. This is what typically leads them into financially overextending themselves.

Are you surprised by all the ways that people can differ in terms of their natural approaches to money—with each person believing his needs, values, and behaviors are "right"? How much conflict have you experienced in your life over money because of personality differences? Who has that conflict been with?

If you are married, has one of those "combatants" been your spouse? When two become as one, they will create a new money personality from the combination of preferences and life experiences of each of the partners. Your money personality will either peacefully coexist or be constantly aggravated by the marriage's money personality. The next chapter will present insights to help spouses accept, appreciate, and accommodate the differences in a way that reduces financial conflict in the marital relationships.

CHAPTER EIGHT

Conquest or Conciliation: Money and Marriage

> Take it from me, marriage isn't a word—it's a sentence.
>
> —*King Vidor*

King Vidor, a famous Hollywood filmmaker, seemed frustrated when he called marriage "a sentence." Marriage can succeed and it offers men and women an opportunity for great joy and personal growth. Clearly, though, marriage will have a profound effect on their finances. When two become as one, they will create a new money personality from the combination of preferences and life experiences of each of the partners. Your own money personality will either peacefully coexist or be constantly aggravated by the marriage's money personality.

According to financial planner and psychologist Victoria Felton-Collins, "90 percent of divorces are caused by money."[1] And while one survey found that seven out of ten couples occasionally disagree on financial issues, other research suggests that *all* marriages have money problems.[2] Perhaps Canadian couples avoid the problem altogether: One study found that 33 percent of them don't even talk about money.[3] It seems that money causes problems with marriage and marriage causes problems with money.

I believe that problems managing money and marriage are a leading contributor to the typical American's financial paradox: increasing wealth leading to increasing financial problems and decreasing financial satisfaction.

DIFFERENT PERSPECTIVES

Picture a husband and wife in their not-so-favorite pastime of thinking about money. One partner sees money pragmatically—as a tool to achieve independence and accomplish goals. The other partner sees money socially—as a tool to achieve intimacy and create community. Both think about money regularly, but when these thoughts turn into words and actions, the partnership becomes imperiled. Because of money, two people who were once in the same boat rowing together are now like two ships passing in the night, each one being rocked by the other's waves. *Seasick* may be the best description for how married couples feel about money talks.

Larry learned this firsthand in one of the biggest arguments that he and his wife Sandy ever had, one they've nicknamed the Furniture Meltdown. Unlike most arguments, this was not over one person wanting to buy something against the other one's wishes. They had both agreed to buy furniture. They had both agreed how much was reasonable to spend. Because they had planned to pay cash, they had agreed on a time frame when such a large purchase would be affordable.

But motivated by a sale ad, Sandy decided they should make the purchase. Larry, however, wasn't ready. In his mind, the price was right but the timing was wrong. The passionate "discussion" over their differences left them both again seasick over money; he had a migraine; she an upset stomach. Why did this happen? How could all of their prior agreements blow up in their faces?

Like many married couples, their money talk was beset by three common conflict creators:

- differences in family history that caused them to see financial issues from different perspectives;
- personality type differences that affected their outlooks, communications, and action; and
- poor relational skills, especially in terms of understanding each other's differences and knowing how to put that

understanding to work in a mutually satisfying manner, irrespective of the eventual outcome.

THE SYMPTOMS:
CONFLICT, CONQUEST, AND CONTROL

Those three causes of conflict are behind a typical marital conflict. Marital conflict happens when the two partners simultaneously pursue mutually exclusive goals. Typically, conflict is resolved by *conquest,* a dominating exercise of power by the person who has the greatest power to inflict their will. *Control* occurs when one party views himself (or herself) as having to go along without choice. Frustration, anger, and resentment are the typical products of this model of interaction.

This is exactly what happened in the Furniture Meltdown between Larry and Sandy. Their quarrel began when the couple realized they had mutually exclusive goals. Spurred by seeing furniture she wanted in a sale ad, Sandy wanted to buy immediately. Larry, looking at their overall financial picture, liked the price but thought the timing was premature.

Different Focuses, Different Decision Processes

Polarized by their opinions as how to resolve this conflict, each began to exert influence on the other. How each one wields influence is primarily an expression of their personalities but also their values and life experiences. Sandy, a dominant sensor, was focused on the immediate and practical so she saw furniture, on sale, *today.* Larry saw what she saw but, being a dominant intuitive, his focus immediately jumped to the big picture of their overall financial status.

Differences in focus were one source of conflict. Another major conflict creator was the differing decision processes. As we saw in chapter 5, men and women tend to have very different preferences while making decisions. Sandy, like most women, is a feeler and values decisions that preserve or create harmony, community, and intimacy.[4] She saw the sale-priced furniture as an opportunity to achieve this right away. Being a feeler, she acknowledged her excitement as a reliable guide to arrive at the conclusion that now was the best time to buy the furniture.

Larry's decision process was quite different. While he certainly cared about his wife's excitement, like most men he preferred to make the decision independently and his wife's legitimate emotions were interfering with that. As a thinker, he preferred to put aside his feelings for his wife's excitement and even his own strong desire for the furniture, in favor of an objective, logical view of the situation. And being a dominant intuitive, he was comfortable with waiting until some future time when, at least in his mind, the timing would be better.

Both Sandy and Larry saw their own view of the situation as right because their individual assessments felt so natural. Ironically, it was as each tried to move closer to the other's side that the conflict escalated from a minor disagreement into open hostility. Like most extraverts, Larry gained energy from intense interactions and tended to confront emotionally difficult situations to work them out or at least discharge their emotions. Sandy, the introvert, naturally drew energy inward and would find herself overloaded if intense negative energy is directed at her. So Larry became increasingly frustrated as Sandy withdrew from the discussion. And Sandy became increasingly uncomfortable as Larry argued with renewed enthusiasm.

Different Personalities

Sandy, a judger, had quickly come to a decision about the furniture based upon what she had seen. Larry, a perceiver, wanted to stay open to other possibilities before reaching a final decision. So he started asking questions in an attempt to gather information that might persuade him to make the purchase now. How long would the sale last? Will it go on sale again and if so, when might that be? Do they have any special financing arrangements?

Besides trying to defend herself against Larry's intense energy, Sandy regarded his impersonal, analytical style of gathering and assessing information as evidence that Larry didn't care about her desires. The more he analyzed the facts, the less she felt that he cared about her facts—how much she wanted the furniture *now*. Translated, "if he doesn't care about this, he doesn't care about me!"

A major cause of Larry and Sandy's differences regarding the furniture was their extreme personality differences. As an ENTP (Larry) and ISFJ (Sandy), they have no personality preferences in common, an unusual occurrence. Most couples share two or more preferences.[5] But regardless of the source, this financial conflict, like many others between married couples, was resolved by conquest. The winner of the conflict was Larry's independent, objective assessment that while this was a good opportunity, it didn't comfortably fit into their overall picture at the present time.

Meet the Conqueror

In this instance, Larry won by conquest. Therefore, they would have to wait and take a chance that they would be able to buy the same furniture at the same price later on when their financial condition allowed.

While sometimes Sandy is the conqueror, in the case of the Furniture Meltdown, Larry had the greatest power to inflict his will on Sandy. Because of economic factors and social conditioning (men "do money," women don't), women are frequently at a disadvantage to men in financial matters. Therefore, it is often the case that men will be the conqueror in financial conflicts. As a result, Sandy felt controlled and angry that, once again, her rights as an equal partner had been appropriated.

Perhaps you've never had a furniture meltdown in your marriage, but chances are you've experienced significant personality-related conflict over something else. Look at the frequently cited money personality conflict creators listed in table 5 on page 136.

Given all the differences that exist between two people in terms of personality, not to mention money memories and financial fallacies—with each person believing that his experiences, attitudes, needs, values, and behaviors are "right"—is it any surprise that there is so much conflict surrounding money in relationships? And given how much money matters, is it any surprise that being controlled in family financial affairs creates so much distress?

Table 5
PERSONALITY CONFLICTS INVOLVING MONEY

Contenders	Conflict
Sensors vs. Intuitives	• Function and engineering vs. Aesthetic beauty and elegance • Knowing what you want and going to get it vs. Not sure what you want but you know it when you see it • Buy now vs. Buy later
Thinkers vs. Feelers	• Buy what I want vs. Having trouble spending money on myself
Protectors vs. Pleasers	• Giving people what they need vs. Giving people what they want or like • Practicality, not quality vs. Quality, not practicality
Protectors vs. Players	• Spending on major, long-lasting, functional purchases vs. Spending on good time, instant gratification, conspicuous consumer purchases
Planners vs. Pleasers	• Life centered around work vs. Life centered around relationships
Players vs. Pleasers	• Materialism and search for good times vs. Spirituality and search for meaning
Protectors vs. Planners	• Tried and true vs. New and improved • Practical, realistic and conservative financial management vs. Imaginative, unproven and risky financial management

If you're married, this is a good point to answer for yourself these two questions about money and your marriage: (1) What are the differences between the ways you and your spouse handle money and make financial decisions? (2) What factors account for these differences: family history, life experience, and/or personality?

THE PROBLEM WITH CONQUEST AND CONTROL

While the conflict, conquest, and control model of interaction seems to be typical for most couples, it is a dysfunctional way to resolve conflict that causes one or both parties to experience debilitating consequences. These consequences are most keenly felt by women because, while they are aware that marital money matters are not being handled in a mutually satisfactory way, they decide that:

- this really shouldn't be a problem to them because their husband doesn't act like it's a problem to him; or
- that there is a problem and because of their more affiliative, cooperative nature, they assume that the problem is them, and they'll continue to make concessions to achieve harmony.

Unfortunately, acting like there isn't a problem or taking sole responsibility for a mutual problem isn't a satisfactory way to avoid conflict. The long-term results of trying to avoid conflict, particularly in financial matters where decisions are so frequent, are emotional stress and poor financial management. The poor state of marriages and financial well-being bear this out. But there is a better method to managing money and marriage than conflict, conquest, and control.

THE CURE: CONCILIATE, COMMUNICATE, AND COOPERATE

Fortunately, the Myers-Briggs Type Indicator and personality theory are able to provide a more functional basis for understanding, bridging, and even appreciating previously irreconcilable individual differences. In addition, an awareness of "cultural" differences such as male-female socialization patterns can create a positive, empathic, and respectful environment that is both mutually edifying and financially productive.

Rather than the wielding of power to resolve conflicts, couples should strive to *conciliate, cooperate,* and *communicate* through the use of personality type. In essence, this means that each party will strive to:

- conciliate, attempting to win their partner over by being an attentive, mature listener;
- communicate, using their partner's "type language" to increase the likelihood that they will be understood, not just heard; and
- cooperate, being a positive influence and using each other's strengths to achieve the best results.

A TIME TO CONCILIATE: THE ROLE OF LISTENING

Seeking Good Communication

Step one is to conciliate. Couples talk about many things and get to know each other in many ways prior to marriage. But their financial needs, wants, and desires rarely get addressed in any depth after they marry. Instead, money presents many opportunities for couples to be surprised that their home suddenly contains competing preconceived notions!

Working through these differences with effective communication is challenging under the best of circumstances—and too much communication occurs under less-than-ideal conditions. Knowledge of personality type is key to improving communication, removing unnecessary barriers to mutually satisfying and productive interactions. It can help us become aware of our own natural styles of conversation and alert us what to expect from others.

Good communication is not talking to get agreement but talking through disagreement. There are two prerequisites that you must have for good money talk and both have significant personality type implications:

1. You must have the patience to listen without interrupting.
2. You must have the maturity to listen wholeheartedly by indicating that you have heard and understood what you heard.

These "must-haves" of effective money talk both point to the quintessential desire of communication: the right to be heard.

"Quick Draw" or Withdraw?

Communication is a reciprocal expenditure of energy between two people, a speaker and a listener. The speaker expends energy by transmitting information in the form of words and body language, including vocal inflection. The listener expends energy by receiving and interpreting the transmission. One of the most frequent impediments to communication is interruption. Interruptions can occur at either the speaker's or listener's end, and they are disruptive because they stop the clear flow of ideas.

There are three main causes of interrupted communication. You and/or your spouse may practice one of them. Communication is interrupted when one party: (1) can't wait to express their point of view and has a "quick draw" response; (2) doesn't like topic of discussion and therefore withdraws themselves from it; or (3) fears being controlled and not getting a chance to be heard, and so withdraws from the communication.

In terms of personality type, differences in orientation of energy (extraversion or introversion) and differences in orientation to the external world (judging or perceiving) have a definite effect on communication interruptions. People who prefer extraversion, for instance, are typically demonstrative, animated talkers who think out loud, developing their ideas as they are talking. Extraverts prefer to communicate face-to-face and will go out of their way to do so, although they do like the immediacy of E-mail communication. In contrast, introverts are generally reflective, low-key talkers who prefer to think things through, verbalizing just the results and not their entire thought process. They prefer to take time to think about their responses, sometime even writing them out even if they are going to respond verbally. They are much more comfortable than extraverts with indirect communication: E-mail, letters, faxes.

Both extraverts and introverts are capable of interrupting communication. Because of their energetic, excitable manner of speaking, extraverts are more likely than introverts to interject—that is, to quick draw—their point of view and interrupt communication. Introverts need time to think before they speak and can be overwhelmed by the energy of forceful conversations. Therefore, introverts are more likely than extraverts to withdraw and interrupt communication. Differences between extraverts and introverts can be especially difficult to negotiate but are quite common. One study found that introverted men tend to marry extraverted women but later have trouble with that style of interaction.[6]

One's orientation to the outer world, whether judging or perceiving, also has an effect on communication interruptions. People who prefer judging focus on closure, getting quickly to the point and stating their opinions in a way that makes it appear that their minds are made up. Perceivers focus on gathering information to generate options, considering many points of view and stating their perspective in a way that makes them seem open to changing their mind—if they have a definite opinion at all!

Again, both judgers and perceivers can interrupt communication. Because they prefer a controlled orderly lifestyle, judgers are less likely to interrupt a discussion than the spontaneous, adaptable perceivers. But judgers' decisiveness and control can be stifling at times, either by withdrawing with a once-and-final opinion, or causing others to withdraw from their control of conversations. On the other hand, spontaneous, quick-draw interjections are a way of life with perceivers, whose constant interruptions can be frustrating enough to cause others to withdraw from conversation.

You probably have a fair idea whether you tend to quick draw or withdraw. If not, ask someone that has observed you in a variety of settings to suggest your tendency. Money talk is likely to be especially intense if one spouse is an extravert *and* a perceiver, and the other spouse is an introvert *and* a judger.

Are You Listening?

The second essential aspect of conciliation is mature listening—the ability to listen wholeheartedly by indicating that you have heard and understood what you heard. Wholehearted listening is empathic listening,[7] being so aware, understanding, and sensitive to what's being said as to vicariously experience the feelings, thoughts, and perceptions of the speaker.

The MBTI preferences of sensing and intuition describe the two ways people gather information. Because our ways of perceiving come natural to us, we assume that what we see are the way things are, and we are quick to challenge the character, competence, or qualifications of anyone who challenges us with another point of view. While the way that two people perceive the world may seem worlds apart, mature listeners are able to see the world from the perspective of the other person.

Mature listening is proactive listening. Experts estimate that 10 percent of our communication is words, 30 percent is sounds and 60 percent body language.[8] To listen wholeheartedly, more of your senses than just hearing must be engaged, and more than just your senses must be engaged—you must also use intuition. Mature listening, then, gives you complete, accurate information, and does any activity need complete, accurate data more than money management? Rather than assume that what's normal to you is the norm, a mature listener seeks to deal *first* with the communicator's reality.

Mature listening requires effort because it means working with your less preferred method of gathering information. Intuitives will naturally be adept at interpreting the inferred aspects of communicating. But they will struggle with engaging their senses and patiently attending to the way sensing types usually talk. People with a preference for sensing talk about the here and now and support their view of present reality with past experience. They are drawn to current practicality, use concrete language, and are quick to provide specific facts, figures, and examples. When talking money with a sensing type, intuitives can expect to hear a lot of details about present needs, how much money is required to meet the need, whether or not the funds are available, and how similar purchases have worked or not worked out in the past.

Listening by Sensors and Intuitives

Sensing types will naturally be adept at interpreting non-verbal aspects of communication. But they will struggle with engaging their intuition and patiently attending to the way intuitives usually talk. People with a preference for intuition talk conceptually about the future and support their view of reality by presenting a vision of what can be. They are drawn to future potential, use abstract language, communicate circuitously (jumping around to connect unrelated points), and are quick to draw associations and figures of speech, but slow to provide specifics. When talking money with an intuitive, sensing types can expect to hear a lot of concepts about future needs, a ballpark estimate of much money may be required to meet the need, and a rough outline of the plan to raise the funds. The intuitive will also explain why his vision of the future is superior to the experiences of the past.

Mature listening begins with an awareness of each other's points of view. If there are differences, they have the potential to broaden the perspective of each partner. If these differences are tolerated, the result can be a balance between two perspectives rather than a destructive contest that eliminates one.

Exercise 9
ARE YOU A SENSING TYPE OR INTUITIVE?

As you read through the overview of your preferred style of communicating, you probably felt validated. And as you read through the opposite preferred style of communicating you probably felt somewhat uncomfortable. Sensing types will be frustrated by the intuitives big picture, "see the forest" point of view and have difficulty following their loopy and leaping style of communicating that doesn't "get to the point." Intuitives will be frustrated by sensing types specific, "see the trees" point of view and have difficulty processing details that seem to go nowhere.

1. To what degree has your preference for sensing or intuition affected your money talk?
2. What do you have to do to be a more mature listener?

Eventually each party in communication must come to a personal decision about what they are hearing. Mature listening is critical to insure that everything that needs to be heard is heard. Sometimes empathic listening is enough to bring two conflicting parties into agreement. But mature listening is not necessarily agreement. It's connecting emotionally as well as verbally. Quite often the goal of money talk is to agree without being disagreeable. Whether you agree or disagree with what you hear involves a decision, which means involving you and your partner's preferences for thinking and feeling.

Listening by Thinkers and Feelers

People who prefer thinking are problem solvers who want to get right down to business. They speak in terms of pros and cons, see the glass half empty, and are quick to make constructive criticism of others' ideas. When talking money with a thinker, you can expect a focus on what's true, the costs and benefits, and the consequences. In general, thinkers prefer to settle disagreements based upon premises that are fair and objective, even if it means that someone will be unhappy.

Exercise 10

ARE YOU A THINKER OR FEELER?

As you read through the opposite preferred style of communicating, you probably felt somewhat uncomfortable. Thinkers will be frustrated by the feeler's subjective, case-by-case point of view and have difficulty using the feeler's emotions as part of the decision-making process. Feelers will be frustrated by the thinker's objective search for a universal truth that applies in all situations and have difficulty having their emotions— which they use as part of their decision-making process—stifled by the thinker's critical nature.

1. To what degree has your preference for thinking or feeling affected your money talk?
2. What do you have to do to be a more mature listener?

People who prefer feeling are harmonizers who focus first on relationships rather than problems. They appreciate and strive to build on the contribution of others' perspectives, see the glass half full and are quick to seek agreement with the ideas of others. Even in conflict, a feeler will typically try to find something to affirm before stating a dissenting opinion. When talking money with a feeler, you can expect to hear the person focus on his interest in principals rather than principle and interest, and the likes and dislikes of people rather than the pros and cons of problems. In general, feelers prefer to make decisions based upon what will create the most goodwill.

Ultimately, mature listening is risky because it makes you vulnerable. By unreservedly opening yourself up to another's values, thoughts, and desires, you allow the possibility that you can be influenced. But whether or not you actually are persuaded to take another point of view, you have taken an important step in reducing marital money conflict by giving your spouse a true gift: the knowledge that they've been heard.

CHAPTER NINE

"Honey, Let's Talk Money!"

> We have to face the fact that either all of us are going to die together or we are going to learn to live together, and if we are to live together we have to talk.
>
> —*Eleanor Roosevelt*

Because money matters, money talk matters. Because money talk matters, mature listening—the type we looked at in chapter 8—matters. *The reason mature listening matters is that it shows your spouse that he or she matters.* Being a good money talker means making your spouse feel validated, fulfilled, affirmed, and appreciated. When your mate feels that way, he or she will be in the best position to hear you.

Listening is the foundation for effective money talk. But effective money talk will always focus on *Step 2: communicate.* Once you have completely gathered and correctly interpreted what was transmitted to you, and evaluated its importance to your partner, good money talk then involves speaking in a way that allows *you* to be just as completely and correctly understood.

Following the axiom of "when in Rome, do as the Romans do," a knowledge of personality type will allow you to speak your partner's language, thereby increasing the likelihood that you will be heard independent of how well they are listening.

A TIME TO COMMUNICATE

Are You an Insider or Outsider?

As we saw in chapter 7, there are four dominant processes—sensing, intuition, thinking, feeling—and you have one that is the governing force of your personality. Each of the four dominant functions is expressed in four different personality types. For example, the four dominant sensors are ESFP, ESTP, ISTJ, and ISFJ. Notice that two of these are extravert (ESFP and ESTP) and two are introvert (ISTJ and ISFJ). While all four types share sensing as the core of their personality, they use their dominant process in one of two different ways: as an expressive extravert or a reflective introvert. Your money will buy even greater happiness if you can talk about it and use it with your preferred "side"—as an insider or as an outsider.

If you are an extravert, your natural inclination is to use your dominant process in the outer world of people, places, and things. If you are an introvert, your natural inclination is to use your dominant process alone, in the inner world of private thoughts and reflection. When interacting with others, extraverts prefer to spontaneously express themselves, and they derive energy from the self-expression of others. Introverts prefer to interact without spontaneous expression, and it is their own thoughts and feelings that provide them with energy.[1] The differences have key implications for marital money talk.

Those who developed personality type theorized that we may have more difficulty with people who use their dominant process in the world opposite from our own.[2] In other words, as an extraverted intuitive (ENTP), I may have more problems relating to an introverted intuitive than my opposite personality type (ISFJ). For example, as an extravert I direct my ideas, inspirations, and enthusiasm at the people I am interacting with. They will know what I'm thinking. An introverted intuitive would direct their ideas, inspirations, and enthusiasm "backstage" and I won't know what they are. In my desire to receive information to respond to, I may increase the intensity of my expression, which would only serve to overload the introvert, causing them to shut down the "conversation" altogether.

146

The ability to talk about money with your mate without conflict is an important factor in your overall satisfaction with money. The level of conflict experienced will be based, in large part, on differences between dominant personality functions. Awareness of this can not only help your relationship through understanding and mutual acceptance, but it can also alleviate major problems in communication. If you are comanaging money in a relationship, an awareness of your partner's style of money management will help you see that they aren't weird; they're just a different kind of normal!

The tips that follow will give you some practical suggestions to improve your effectiveness in talking money with each of the four dominant types. What is true for the dominant types is also true for nondominant types, but to a lesser degree. For instance, nondominant sensors (ISTP, ISFP, ESTJ, ESFJ) will exhibit many, or all, of the same sensing behaviors as dominant sensors. However, the greatest differences between people in terms of financial behaviors appear to be along the lines of their dominant processes.

HOW TO TALK MONEY ACCORDING TO YOUR MATE'S DOMINANT PROCESS

How to Talk Money with a Dominant Sensor

The dominant sensor is either an ISTJ, ISFJ, ESTP, or ESFP personality type. If your spouse or you determine that he/she is a dominant sensor, use the following strategies when it's time to talk money matters:

1. *"Just the facts, ma'am."* You must appreciate the sensor's love for detail. Don't digress or change subjects and don't overwhelm the sensor with extraneous information. She'll get annoyed and start tuning you out.

2. *Begin at the beginning.* Start with the details, then move to a discussion of the goal. "You know the overtime you're working this week? Let's use it to take a weekend trip. We both need a break."

3. *Be concrete.* Say exactly what you mean and use adjectives sparingly and carefully. Don't exaggerate or generalize

with sensors as they are very literal communicators. They can be distrustful of information that cannot be readily observed.

4. *Show practicality.* You must demonstrate and justify to them how any expense will be used to meet a specific need. Usefulness today is more important than future possibilities.

5. *Determine whether they are introverts or extraverts,* and respond accordingly. Remember, introvert dominant sensors (ISTJ and ISFJ) are managers of facts and details. In conversation, they like things kept factual and stated clearly and simply. Support their desire to be responsible and their capacity for noticing details and making practical observations about them. In contrast, extravert dominant sensors (ESTP and ESFP) are adapters. Open-minded and tolerant, they accept what they see and hear, and adapt accordingly. Support their desire to adapt to or even change present circumstances, and to experience and enjoy life.

How to Talk Money with a Dominant Intuitive

The dominant intuitive is either an INTJ, INFJ, ENTP, or ENFP personality type. If your spouse or you determine that the other is a dominant intuitive, use the following strategies when it's time to talk money matters:

1. *Start with the end in mind.* Start with the goal and then move to a discussion of the details. "Let's take a weekend trip. We both need a break. We can use the money from the overtime you're working this week." (Compare this to the same comments made to a sensor, above.)

2. *Get their attention by asking questions or throwing out possibilities.* "You want to go to that bed and breakfast that the Bruces liked so much? Or would you rather go to the beach? Maybe I can get off on Friday and we can make it a long weekend."

3. *Talk in "chunks" and not in details.* Intuitives' eyes begin to glaze over and their minds start to wander when things get down to the nitty-gritty details. It's best to talk about

148

broad issues—vacation, retirement, home renovation—
and let their imagination fill in the blanks.

4. *Motivate them with the possibility of future change.* To an intuitive, things can always be better! Even if it's not broken, an intuitive will still want to fix it. Start a question
   with, "I wonder if . . .", or, "I wonder how . . .", then get
   out of their way.

5. *Keep in mind whether they are an introvert or an extravert.*
   The dominant intuitives who are introverts (INTJ and
   INFJ) are also "innovators"—imaginative, ingenious, and
   independent minded. They will listen to what others
   have to say but refuse to be coerced by it. Support them
   by appreciating the depth and excellence of their insight.
   Meanwhile, extravert dominant intuitives (ENTP and
   ENFP) are "change agents." Charming and energetic, their
   infatuation with possibilities can sometimes be stimulating and sometimes overwhelming. Support their enthusiasm for inspiring ideas (ENTP) or ideals (ENFP) and
   their unquenchable desire to learn.

How to Talk Money with a Dominant Thinker

Just as it is very difficult to continue a discussion when two
parties start with different perspectives, it can be hard to reach
agreement if they have differing decision styles. Feelers tend
to focus on areas of agreement while thinkers tend to concen-
trate on areas of disagreement. With about 65 percent of men
being thinkers and about 65 percent of women being feelers,
many money talk conflicts will occur because of differences between these two styles of making decisions. What follows may
be helpful in terms of communicating to your thinking spouse
(who is ISTP, INTP, ESTJ, or ENTJ).

1. *Know why.* "I need some extra money because . . ."

2. *Listen to what they say, not how they say it.* Thinkers pride
   themselves on saying *precisely* what they mean. There are
   no hidden agendas; therefore feelers should not read anything else into their conversations—it makes thinkers crazy.

3. *Don't personalize their comments.* "You spent too much this week on groceries," doesn't mean they think you're a bad person, it's just a statement of fact to a thinker.

4. *Keep your emotions in check.* Thinkers only want to expend energy solving problems, not "waste" energy dealing with your emotions. They will tend to avoid issues or decisions if they fear an emotional outburst is forthcoming.

5. *Determine whether they are an introvert or an extravert.* Introverts (ISTP and INTP) are "analyzers." Expect them to consider the social and emotional domains of life inferior to long-term accomplishments in the mental domain, but they may have difficulty in conveying their decisions to others with warmth and respect. Support their *logical analysis* by responding to the underlying realities (ISTP) or principles (INTP) involved in a discussion. In contrast, *extraverts* (ESTJ and ENTJ) are "organizers." Anticipate their impulses to make decisions for the sake of making decisions, inside or outside their fields of expertise. Support their desire to take charge by organizing, regulating, and directing action (ESTJ) or change (ENTJ).

How to Talk Money with a Dominant Feeler

The dominant feeler is either an ISFP, INFP, ESFJ, or ENFJ personality type. If your spouse or you determine that the other is a dominant feeler, use the following strategies when it's time to talk money matters:

1. *Give plenty of verbal affirmation.* Feelers thrive on praise and encouragement for them, not what they do. Tell them, "You're a great shopper," instead of, "Thanks for staying under budget."

2. *Put yourself, not the information, into the conversation.* Begin statements with, "I feel good when . . .", rather than "The right thing to do is . . ."; or "It hurts me when . . .", as opposed to "This is terrible."

3. *Don't debate, validate.* To feelers, a conversation is not just an exchange of information but a sharing of a life. "Mirror" their feelings before you respond and then show a

mutual interest in the problem. Thus, when a feeler tells you, "We never have money to go out anymore," acknowledge before you answer. "I know you feel like we never have the money to go out. Perhaps we should sit down together and work out a new spending plan."

4. *Do things with, not for.* Don't just give her a spending plan—help her spend it! Feelers want to do things with people rather than having things done for them. Know what her primary interests are, how to finance them and then, enjoy participating with her.

5. *Determine whether they are an introvert or an extravert,* and respond accordingly. Introverts (ISFP and INFP) are helpers. They reserve their rich reservoir of warmth and enthusiasm for those few people they care deeply about. Show them support by encouraging and being engaged in their desire to contribute to the personally meaningful value-driven *causes* (ISFP) or *potential* for people (INFP) that matter to them. Meanwhile, extraverts (ESFJ and ENFJ) are "harmonizers." Communicate to them with warmth and companionship. Support their desire to satisfy the *tangible needs* (ESFJ) or *ideals* (ENFJ) for the people and institutions they value.

Exercise 11

ARGUMENTS AND PERSONALITY TYPE

Refer to you and your spouse's personality type and think back to an argument you've had over money. Then answer these questions:

1. Are there differences in communication style between sensing and intuition, thinking and feeling, or both?
2. How could have that interaction been different if you had taken their preferred communication style into account?
3. How can you modify your communication style to be heard better by your spouse?

Understanding others is the gateway to human excellence. When you use awareness of personality type in any interpersonal relationships, you are recognizing and respecting another person's preference and allowing him to receive communication in a "language" that is most natural to him.

It is the appreciation of what is praiseworthy in each other that matters most, and expressing that appreciation in communication enhances relationships, improves cooperation, and makes life with your partner much more enjoyable. It does require effort, but learning to communicate in your partner's language is an investment that is sure to return dividends.

A TIME TO COOPERATE

Consider the benefits of consulting all four major types. A practical view of a situation comes from a sensor. A vision of the future comes from an intuitive. Objective analysis comes from a thinker. Concern for how a situation will affect people comes from a feeler. A good decision requires the right input at the right time from *each* type. The challenge is to allow each other's inputs to become part of the solution and not part of the problem. After conciliation, and then communication, you can become more helpful to your spouse if you modify your behavior to *cooperate* with them through their personality preferences.

Moving Beyond Conflict

Step three for effective money talk is cooperate. Cooperation is the opposite of conflict, where two parties self-centeredly and simultaneously pursue mutually exclusive goals. With cooperation, two parties try to reach a mutually satisfying outcome; each is willing to sacrifice. With conflict, the goal is to defend your point of view by attacking that of the other party. With cooperation, the goal is to protect a portion of the other's point of view by sacrificing a portion of your own.

Cooperation occurs in an environment where two parties see their personality type differences as mutually beneficial rather than competing.

This does not mean that you completely abandon your own preferences nor does it mean that you are manipulating your partner through false appearances. On the contrary, in a cooperative "type" of environment, each partner feels secure enough to interact on the level of his spouse's natural strengths instead of his own. It's when two people approach a problem with different interests, values, and problem-solving techniques that they see things not obvious to the other. Use of personality type can allow partners to complement each other and be able to expose any aspect of an issue that has been overlooked.

This will require you to know how the personality strengths of your partner interact with the needs of your own personality type. It is very useful for each of you to recognize your limitations and how the preferences of your spouse will help you to see all the sides of an issue. To allow your natural skills to work with your spouse's, you need to be open to how your marriage partner can be your financial friend rather than a fiscal foe.

Creating a Cooperative Environment

The first step in working together is to create a cooperative environment. You can use your partner's MBTI preferences that relate to energy flow (extravert/introvert) and lifestyle (judger/perceiver) to provide your spouse with a cooperative environment where they can operate with the greatest ease and satisfaction. Table 6 on the next page offers some helpful hints.

How to Be a Terrific Teammate

If a spouse is going to be open to allowing her partner to help her make decisions, then that partner should know the best way to do that. She needs to know enough about her spouse to be able to effectively give and receive the spouse's help. As alluded to in discussing communication, good problem solving involves the sequential use of four processes.

When faced with a financial problem, the best place to start is a realistic view of the facts. Sensing is the best process for this. The relationship of the facts and to other relevant information should come next. Intuition is the best process for this. Armed with possibilities, the thinking process analyzes the logical consequences of acting on each alternative. Finally, these possibilities need to be evaluated for their consequences to the people involved.

Table 6

HOW TO RECEIVE COOPERATION

To Get the Most Cooperation from Extraverts	To Get the Most Cooperation from Introverts
They thrive on energy, so be energetic and enthusiastic	They resist energy, so tone down energy and enthusiasm
Strive for an immediate reaction— and then be ready for it	Don't force them to take immediate action—allow them time to consider their response
Don't assume their talking is their final answer— allow them to think out loud	Don't assume their silence means agreement—draw them out
They equate immediacy with importance, so interrupt them if you want their attention	Give advanced warning that you need to talk and, if possible, give them something to read over first

To Get the Most Cooperation from Judgers	To Get the Most Cooperation from Perceivers
Have a clear and agreed upon purpose for a discussion	Adapt to a flexible agenda and prepare to explore tangential (or even unrelated) issues
Strive for closure on a decision— and then keep it closed, even in the face of new data	If new data becomes available, be ready to review a prior decision
Express views definitively	Express views tentatively

It didn't go well for Larry when he got another one of his hot flashes of inspiration. With great energy and enthusiasm, he suggested to Sandy his innovative idea for a home-based business. As usual, he presented it in his typically sketchy fashion, assuming that his wife would excitedly catch the vision enough to ignore the still vague details. Unfortunately, his sensing wife did not react to the concept, but rather to the missing details and therefore rejected the idea as unworkable—which it was in its present, unfinished form. The result was no new business, just wounded feelings.

An awareness and appreciation of personality type could have made the intuitive's dream a sensor's reality, if the listener—in this case Sandy the Sensor—had given Larry the Intuitive's idea a chance. She could have used her assessment skills and experience to force her intuitive husband to fill in the blanks by asking questions like, "What would you do about . . .", "When do you plan to . . .", or "How will you handle . . ." Loving a challenge, the intuitive would probably have risen to the occasion and generated enough ideas to create a workable solution—and then let the sensor help him manage the business! With their different personality types and a cooperative spirit, each partner should do what they do best. Table 7 on page 156 contains other suggestions for how sensors and intuitives can help each other.

Likewise, we each have needs when it comes to making decisions. Again, what we know about ourselves will allow our partners to be excellent teammates. As you read through the lists in table 7, see yourself in the role of a teammate or partner. Which of these describe you? Which describe your spouse?

When two people become one despite all of the differences in their memories, experiences, and personalities, it can be a daunting task to make it all work, and it would appear that working together on the family finances is the most daunting task of all. How should we respond to conflict between two points of view caused by personality-type differences? One or both partners have to make a choice as to what they believe. They can:

- self-righteously put their spouse down by believing that it is wrong for them to be different;
- self-deprecatingly believe that they are the cause of the conflict because it is wrong for them to be different from their spouse;
- self-centeredly demand their own way no matter what;
- hopelessly believe that, although they are probably OK as individuals, they are poorly suited for each other because they never seem to agree on anything.

Table 7
HELPING EACH OTHER

How Intuitives Can Help Sensors	How Sensors Can Help Intuitives
Sharing their ingenuity	Sharing their experience
Showing them a vision—"What can be" to prepare them for the future (investing, saving); and	Showing them details—"What is" to help them meet present needs (pay bills, track spending plans, stay on top of repairs and maintenance);
Helping them make strategic, long-range plans like investment strategies and debt reduction plans	Keeping them accountable for day-to-day tasks, such as keeping organized records and managing the checkbook
Encouraging them to anticipate the joys of spending money in the future—next year's vacation, retirement	Encouraging them to experience the joys of spending money in the present: "Let's go out to eat tonight."
Showing them that "when there's a will there's a way"	Showing them that "a stitch in time saves nine"
Helping them to loosen up and "chill out"	Helping them get their head "out of the clouds"

How Feelers Can Help Thinkers	How Thinkers Can Help Feelers
Helping them to appreciate their feelings	Helping them to analyze situations
Helping them to promote harmony among people	Helping them to be assertive with salespeople
Helping them to affirm people's feelings during a move	Helping them to affirm the tangible benefits of a move
Helping them to see money as a tool for people—insurance, college saving, charitable giving	Helping them to see money as a tool in a process—cutting taxes, reducing debt, improving cash flow
Encouraging them to deal warmly with family relationships	Encouraging them to deal coolly with sensitive family business
Helping them to see the family as providing true support of their financial objectives	Helping them to organize the family to achieve their financial objectives

None of these offers a positive outcome. There is only one belief that can make you and your spouse fiscal friends rather than financial foes. *You must believe that you and your partner are justifiably and interestingly different from each other, respecting those unique differences and affirming your need for your spouse's gifts in your life.*

Your greatest personal satisfaction and contribution to your partner will come when you choose to work with, rather than against, the diversity of your personality types. The result can be a partnership that has the potential to be mutually rewarding for both parties. When marriage partners will bridge the gap between their differences with conciliation, communication, and cooperation, instead of conflict, conquest, and control, they will be able to manage their money and their marriage more effectively—and more enjoyably, too!

CHAPTER TEN

Suit Yourself to a Custom-Tailored Career

Set me in a task in which I can put something of my very self, and it is a task no longer; it is joy, it is art.

—*Bliss Carman*

Just like most other living things, grass needs water to live and grow. I am reminded of this fundamental truth as I look at our browned and patchy lawn, dried up from lack of water due to the midsummer drought conditions we are experiencing. No matter that we have spent considerable time, energy, and money to have thriving green grass. Without water, our lawn cannot attain the full, lush potential that it was intended to have.

Because of the extraordinarily dry conditions, our lawn found itself out of its natural element, in an environment it never planned to be in. If the lawn could have replanted itself elsewhere, it no doubt would have. But in these unfamiliar conditions, its life ebbed away. It simply dried up, as there was just not enough vitality in the environment to sustain it.

I see our lawn as a metaphor for a job or career. Like grass, people find it easy to thrive in work settings that are natural to them, that give them life and sustenance. But many people find themselves in working environments that are unnatural. Just as with the resources we put into our lawn, they have spent much time, energy, and money to "grow" a career, only to find their careers dried up. Like the grass that strives mightily, but in vain, to grow without water, many are struggling in their work because they, too, are not being nourished by the conditions around them.

FINDING TRUE JOB SATISFACTION

If you have a career, most of your life will be spent working for pay. Too many people, regardless of income level, have found that their financial compensation was not enough to make up for the dissatisfaction of unfulfilling jobs. After years of study, thousands of dollars of education, and working eight hours or more a day year after year at jobs that do not provide happiness, they found themselves feeling like the parched lawn, wondering if and when they will ever achieve the potential promised by the investments they've made in their careers.

Nobody ever plans to make a less-than-satisfying career choice. Yet it appears that many people do just that. In one survey, 48 percent of middle managers confessed that their "lives were empty and meaningless." Paradoxically, higher levels of success were even more disappointing. Better than two out of every three senior executives, 68 percent, similarly concluded that "their lives were empty and meaningless."[1]

However, unlike our burned-out lawn, anyone who is unhappy in their work can choose a different environment to work in. But how will that choice be made? The world of money is full of information on how to plan your finances. Unfortunately, there is a lot less information available on how to plan to earn your finances! Just as your knowing your money personality can help you happily spend money, it can help you happily earn it, too.

Doing What You Most Enjoy

Simply stated, the easiest way to attain career success and experience job satisfaction is to do what you enjoy the most. King Solomon wisely observed that if a person is happy in his work, he "seldom reflects on the days of his life, because God keeps him occupied with gladness of heart"[2] The perfect job is fulfilling because it affords you ample opportunities to express your natural talents, to do things that you find valuable, and to satisfy your core needs. Like a custom tailored suit, it fits who you are better than a job picked "off the shelf" when you needed to work.

In the right job you should:

- look forward to going to work;
- feel energized (most of the time) by what you do;
- feel your contribution is respected and appreciated;
- feel proud when describing your work to others;
- enjoy and respect the people you work with; and
- feel optimistic about your future.[3]

Most people in the right job will experience less stress, greater satisfaction, and higher productivity over the long run.

Perhaps at some point you have had such a job, or one at least somewhat gratifying. Complete exercise 12 to recall your experience and response to that environment.

Exercise 12

MY FAVORITE JOB OR TASK

Take some time to think about your favorite job or the most enjoyable or successful project that you ever worked on.

Write on a piece of paper:

- the nature of the job or project
- the skills you found yourself using
- why you felt it was so enjoyable

Reflect on your answers to exercise 12. Keep in mind that because the answers for each criterion differ for individuals, there is no ideal job that everybody should desire. Nor are there financial requirements that define the right job. But the ideal job for each person does exist, and your money personality can help lead you to it. Considering your personality type is of great advantage in making career choices because the energy for succeeding in your work comes from exercising your innate type preferences. Years of MBTI research has shown that people are attracted to those careers that allow them to make use of the innate type personality type preferences. Therefore, it makes sense to look for your ideal career by looking at jobs that make significant use of your natural giftings.

Any type of work can be broken down into four basic activities. The two primary activities are information gathering and decision making. The two secondary activities are personal contact and goal setting. If these activities sound similar to the Myers-Briggs preference categories, that is because these essential job activities have powerful personality type implications.

Using Your Talents

According to Richard Bolles, the author of the best-selling *What Color is My Parachute?*, we each have been gifted by God to accomplish something specific. Our mission in life is to exercise that talent in settings that appeal to us the most.[4] Using one's greatest gifts, those one delights most in using, is what King Solomon must have had in mind when he wrote, "When God gives any man wealth and possessions, and enables him to enjoy them, to accept his lot and be happy in his work—this is a gift of God.[5]

Popular books with titles such as *Do What You Love and the Money Will Follow* and *Do What You Are* express this idea of working in harmony with our natural talents. The exciting thing is that your talents can be discovered and when you do discover them, you will hold the keys to finding a career that you can work at enthusiastically. If the idea of working with enthusiasm excites you, recognize that the word *enthusiasm* comes from the Greek words *en theos*, meaning "with God." Given the root meaning of *enthusiasm* and *realizing* what Bolles and Solomon have said about work, it should come as no surprise that we should be so fulfilled by work that uses our God-given talents in settings where He has made us to flourish.

TEMPERAMENT AND CAREER

Understanding your temperament can help you predict behavior preferences and patterns. This is because your behavior patterns are simply a reflection of using your natural gifts, according to a deeply held system of personal values, to meet the inner needs of your inborn personality. Therefore, knowing your temperament can be a very good tool for providing career guidance. Given the amount of our lives spent at work, our jobs present a wonderful opportunity to spend time in a personally fulfilling line of work, regardless of the income derived from it.

Protectors, players, pleasers, and planners have very different and distinct career interests. Depending on circumstances, skill level, desire, or maturity, each temperament may succeed at jobs they are not necessarily ideally suited for. Human behavior is far too complex to guarantee outcomes in any setting. You should not be discouraged from pursuing an occupation that you are not the "perfect" personality for. You may be able to make valuable contributions to your work in an unconventional way or enjoy the challenge of stretching the limits of your capabilities.

Because our enthusiasm for work can be so closely related to temperament, it is important to discuss how job performance and satisfaction are affected by each of the four temperament patterns. The illustrations below are overviews of the kind of vocational missions each temperament appears to be uniquely created for.

Protectors (SJ): Working for Usefulness

Sensing types trust documented experience. Judgers prefer a structured personal environment. Together, these preferences form the combination of the sensing judger—the protector—that is known for contributing predictability, dependability, and timely output. Protectors are responsible, loyal, and industrious. Their work motto could be, "Early to bed and early to rise makes a man healthy, wealthy, and wise."

Although protectors are found in all jobs, they gravitate toward careers that involve creating structure, controls, or conservation. Serious and hardworking, protectors have high expectations of themselves and others. They prefer to work in a structured, stable, and predictable environment that respects the chain of command and where they can expect steadily increasing levels of responsibility. They like to be evaluated by established rules and explicit criteria and then be appreciated for their hard work and ability to get things done in an efficient and organized way. If these rules and criteria are unsatisfactory, they will make better ones. They are often found in large numbers in business, administration, teaching, health care, the military, and the judicial system.

Work situations that protectors can find burdensome are those that involve theories, long-range planning, change, and trying new approaches.

Players (SP): Working for Impact via Action

Again, sensing types trust documented experience. Perceivers prefer to be spontaneous and able to go with the flow. Together, these preferences form the combination of the sensing perceiver—the player—that is known for contributing tactical responsiveness and expeditious handling of the unusual and unexpected. Protectors are clever and timely. Their work motto could be, "Make hay while the sun shines."

While found in all jobs, players tend to derive satisfaction from work that includes a great deal of variety and change, where each day is different and presents fresh challenges. They like to make work fun and therefore enjoy flexible, relaxed work environments without a lot of bureaucracy and rules. Players prefer work that is immediately practical and delivers tangible results. And they like working with real things, often excelling with tools, crafts, or artisanship. Players like challenges and are usually at their best in a crisis. They make great "firefighters," both the kind who put out real fires and those who work for companies to immediately solve important problems as they arise. Careers that attract a large number of players include craftsmanship, performing arts and entertainment, law enforcement, and sports.

Work situations that players can find burdensome are those that involve intangibles and abstractions, or become predictable and lose their novelty after an initial phase of enthusiasm.

Pleasers (NF): Working for Growth

Intuitives are interested in creative possibilities. Feelers prefer to make decisions by considering the impact on people. Together, these preferences form the combination of the intuitive feeler—the pleaser—that is known for contributing personal encouragement and a special vision of possibilities for people. Pleasers interact with people about values and inspirations Their likely work motto is, "Be all that you can be."

Pleasers, like people of the other temperaments, are found in all fields, but they tend to gravitate toward work that inspires people to pursue their passions and develop their potential. Careers that use their natural talents to understand and connect with people is what pleasers find most personally meaningful and rewarding. They need to believe in their work and to be able to see the positive impact it has on others' lives. Pleasers like collegial and conflict-free work environments, working with enthusiastic, caring people where they feel appreciated and liked. Pleasers especially enjoy expressing their idealism by creatively solving problems with global or far-reaching implications, as it allows them and others to fulfill their dreams. Careers that attract large numbers of pleasers are: counseling, social work, ministry, marketing, consulting, and human resources.

Work situations that pleasers can find burdensome are those that are bureaucratic and tightly supervised, that lack enthusiasm, teamwork, and provide little opportunity for professional or personal growth.

Planners (NT): Working for Excellence in Ideas

Again, intuitives are interested in creative possibilities. Thinkers prefer to make decisions based upon impersonal logic and analysis. Together, these preferences form the combination of the intuitive thinker—the planner—that is known for contributing a pursuit of excellence through strategies and analysis. Their work motto could be, "He who stops being better stops being good."

Planners, like the other three temperaments, are found in all jobs. However, they are frequently found in technology and science, or any field that demands high levels of intellectual mastery. Naturally innovative, they enjoy mastering technology and systems to creatively solve complex or theoretical problems. Planners are ambitious, so they prefer environments where they can be evaluated against objective and competitive standards, where breakthroughs are expected to be highly rewarded. They are the most independent of all the temperaments, respecting competence rather the chain of command. Above all, planners need constant stimulation in the form of persistent intellectual growth. Since they like working on new and original projects, they are best at perfecting flawed systems in ingenious ways and then moving on to their next creative challenge. Careers that planners find attractive include: executive-level management, consulting, technology, law, strategic or systems planning, and college professor, especially those in the liberal arts and science.

Work situations that planners can find burdensome are those that accept mediocre performance, lack competitive standards and intellectual creativity, and are resistant to change and innovation.

CHOOSING A JOB

The Role of Perception

One study reported by Isabel Briggs found that the personality type function that indeed has the most influence on occupational choice is perception—sensing or intuition—which determines where one's interests will tend to lie.[6] Sensing types are attracted to situations that have a constant stream of facts. Intuitives prefer those where they can consider possibilities.

Your preference for sensing (S) or intuition (N) deals with how you prefer to gather information, obviously an essential element of any assignment. Awareness of this preference is helpful for identifying what kind of work is probably most initially appealing to you. Table 8 describes what types of work each preference tends to be attracted to, especially if it is your dominant process.

Table 8
STRENGTHS OF THE PERCEIVERS

Sensors	Intuitives
"Carpe Diem." ("Seize the day.")	"Building a better tomorrow."
Doing	Thinking
Hands-on	Imagination
Routine	Creativity
Constant stream of facts	Situations full of possibilities
Stability	Inspiration
Production measured by short-term results	Production measured by long-term results

The last distinction above is very interesting, that of the preference for outcomes that are either short-term or long-term. Sensors tend to favor work that has near-term results while intuitives are very comfortable with outcomes that are measured over the long-term. This can create a distinction among jobs in the same career field. For instance, within the field of finance, one can expect sensors to be drawn to accounting, while intuitives might be drawn to financial planning. In the law field, you will find more sensors in trial law and more intuitives in law school professorates. In engineering, there are more sensors in civil engineering than architectural engineering. Clearly sensors lean more to jobs with measurable results than do the intuitives. For instance, I once surveyed fourteen workers (including the owner) of a local print shop and found all but one was a sensing type. That made sense, as a print shop is clearly a sensing environment: hands-on, routine, constant work with measurable short-term output.

The Role of Decision Making

The next most important function in terms of occupational choice is the kind of judgment that is the most natural and effective to use—thinking or feeling. Thinkers are skilled at handling matters that deal with inanimate objects, machinery, principles, or theories, all of which can be analyzed and handled with logic and objectivity. Feelers are better suited to matters involving people, what they feel and how they can be served or persuaded.

The next primary work activity is decision making. Your preference for thinking or feeling relates to how you make decisions, another fundamental element of all work. Understanding this preference is profitable for finding jobs that call for making judgments in a way that is comfortable and agreeable to you. The table below describes what types of judgments each preference finds most natural, especially if it is your dominant process.

Table 9

STRENGTHS OF THE DECISION MAKERS

Thinkers	Feelers
"Use your head."	"You gotta have heart."
Matters of principle	Matters of persuading
Environment involving process, data, or things	Environment involving people
Decide after objectively considering the results of analysis	Decide after subjectively considering the effect on people
Consistent, logical environments	Inconsistent or unpredictable environments

WHAT'S YOUR SECOND FAVORITE PROCESS?

Recall from chapter 7 that your dominant process is your best developed and most used process. Of the four processes—sensing, intuition, thinking, and feeling—one exerts a governing influence on your behavior. It is the most important and most used part of your personality. This one process alone, however, is not enough. To be well-balanced, we need adequate assistance from a supporting function. Your *auxiliary* function is your second favorite process and plays an essential role in your personality type by providing complementary support to your dominant process.

Spotting your secondary process is easy. If your dominant process is a judging one (thinking or feeling) then your auxiliary is a perceiving one (either sensing or intuition). Likewise, if your dominant process is a perceiving one (either sensing or intuition) then your auxiliary is a judging one (thinking or feeling).

Regardless of your preference for perception, you need to engage your judgment process. Otherwise, dominant sensors would collect facts but arrive at no conclusions about them; dominant intuitives would preoccupy themselves with flights of fancy without ever actually taking flight. If you are unable to move from information gathering to decision making, the result is chronic procrastination and paralyzing indecisiveness.

Those whose dominant function is either thinking or feeling need to ensure that they are not so driven to make decisions without gathering all the necessary information. Without support from a perceiving process, they can become dogmatic, close-minded, and inflexible, regardless of whether they make their decisions according to logical principles or personal priorities.

People should give careful consideration to what jobs and careers would make the best use of their dominant preference of perception (sensing or intuition) or judgment (thinking or feeling), although they are likely to have good (but prehaps not as good) results in jobs that emphasize the use of their auxiliary function. Table 10 indicates the dominant and secondary (auxiliary) process for all sixteen personality types. Consult it as you complete exercise 13.

Table 10

YOUR SECONDARY [AUXILIARY] PROCESS

(The dominant process is shown in boldface.)

ISTJ Thinking	ISFJ Feeling	INFJ Feeling	INTJ Thinking
ISTP Sensing	ISFP Sensing	INFP Intuition	INTP Intuition
ESTP Thinking	ESFP Feeling	ENFP Feeling	ENTP Thinking
ESTJ Sensing	ESFJ Sensing	ENFJ Intuition	ENTJ Intuition

Exercise 13

SPOTTING YOUR
DOMINANT AND SECONDARY PROCESS

Copy your four-letter personality type from chapter 5 in the blanks below.

___ ___ ___ ___

Next, locate the code in table 10. Which is your dominant process and which is your secondary? Dominant: ____ Secondary: ____.

List the opposite letters of these two: ____ ____. These are your inferior processes and work that emphasizes them probably should be avoided.

Your greatest assets are reflected in your dominant and auxiliary functions. They are a vital part of your earning plan as they are the roots through which it is fed. When you are working with your best processes, you have the potential to complete assignments with enthusiasm *(en theos)* in work that is personally stimulating and satisfying. By contrast, it is stressful and depleting to constantly work in an unsuitable environment where your personality is not being nourished. Although no job is perfect, your productivity and satisfaction will usually be highest if you are using your preferred personality processes most of the time.

WHERE IS THE BEST PLACE
TO BE YOUR BEST?

People function best when they can work in an environment that allows them to express the best of their personalities. In addition to preferred types of work, we each have preferred work settings. As previously indicated, highly energized, enthusiastic work will most likely occur when we use our God-given talents in environments where they can flourish. Just like with our specific job assignments, we will experience difficulty working outside of our personality framework. While we normally find using our preferences energizing, using our nonpreferences is typically burdensome. "Frustrating" and "exhausting" are two words often uttered by people when I ask them what it would be like to have a job where they had to write with their nondominant hand. About such an assignment, one person said, "I'd kill somebody!"

Extraverts and Introverts

We've discussed the first two basic work (and life) activities of gathering information and making decisions. The third basic work activity is personal contact. While personal contact may be considered a secondary job activity as compared to information gathering and decision making, all work eventually requires some amount of contact with people.

Your preference for extraversion or introversion is indicative of whether you tend to be an initiator of activity or a responder to activity, and how much contact with other people you are comfortable with. Recall from chapter 5 (and exercise 13) the first letter of your personality type, either E or I. This points to the amount of personal contact you are comfortable

171

with. Extraverts clearly like more contact than introverts. The opposite letter represents the level of personal contact you are least comfortable with; that amount of personal contact probably should be avoided.

The table below describes some job tasks that each preference tends to be most comfortable with.

Table 11

EXTRAVERTS AND INTROVERTS' JOB TASK PREFERENCES

Extraverts	Introverts
Action—initiating, going at a situation to move it forward	Reflection—responding, going away from a situation to contemplate it
Working in teams or task forces	Working alone on solo projects
Motivating	Concentrating
Bullpens	Cubicles
Meetings	Faxes, E-mail, voice mail
Influencing	Listening

Judgers and Perceivers

The final basic activity of work is goal setting. Our preference for judging or perceiving influences the way we set goals, which in turn affects our work habits. Table 12 describes some characteristics of jobs that each preference tends to be most comfortable with.

Recall from chapter 5 (and exercise 13) the last letter of your personality type, either J or P. This points to the kind of work habits that are most natural to you. The opposite letter represents the kind of work habits that are least natural to you; work that is arranged this way probably should be avoided.

Table 12
JUDGERS AND PERCEIVERS'
JOB TASK PREFERENCES

Judgers	Perceivers
Reaching closure	Keeping channels of information open
Plan your work and work your plan	Go with the flow
Feel support from schedules and structure	Feel inhibited by schedules and structure
Explicit plans, probably on paper	Implicit plans, probably "in head"
Running on schedule	Flying by "seat of the pants"
Completing: enjoying the ends	Process: enjoying the means

Optimum Working Conditions

The combination of our first two MBTI letters can help us find our optimum work settings, environments whose work style closely matches our own. Everyone will tend to do their best work in one of the following four situations:

IS (Introversion-Sensing): "Let's keep it!" With a focus on practical considerations, this type of work setting will be attractive to individuals whose natural inclination is to preserve what has proven itself to work, resisting novel and unproven ideas in favor of continuing to rely on past experience.

IN (Introversion-Intuition): "Let's think about it differently!" With a focus on intangible thoughts and details, this type of work setting will be attractive to individuals whose natural inclination is questioning the tried and true, contemplating the future, and looking for ways to make things better than they are today.

ES (Extraversion-Sensing): "Let's do it!" With a focus on practical action, this type of work setting will be attractive to individuals whose natural inclination is practical action, doing what needs to be done, staying on track, and getting results.

EN (Extraversion-Intuition): "Let's change it!" With a focus on systems and relationships, this type of work setting will be attractive to individuals whose natural inclination is to create change, take risks, and constantly evolve in a quest for "new and improved".[7]

Exercise 14

YOUR OPTIMAL WORK ENVIRONMENT

Look up the first and second letters of your Myers-Briggs personality type (shown in exercise 13), and place them here: ____ ____. These represent your optimal work environment, as described above.

Now fill in the opposite letters (either E or I and S or N): ____ ____. These point to your least optimal work environment, and work conditions that emphasize them probably should be avoided.

PLANNING—AND CHANGING—A CAREER

About Burnout

If you're realistic about your job, you'll admit that there are both good days and bad days, no matter how much you love your work. There are challenging and difficult times in every job to overcome. But when you catch yourself thinking, "My job just isn't fun anymore," it could be a sign that you are enduring through the hard times rather than prevailing over them.

"Burnout" is the popular expression that is used to describe the loss of physical, mental, and emotional energy. The term originally was used to describe machinery that was worn out from excessive or improper use. It is the excessive, improper use of the skills inherent in one's personality that can be a primary contributor to job-related burnout.

I used to work with someone named Bill who would say, "I look forward to Fridays like most people look forward to retirement!" While a weekend off is certainly worth looking forward to, obviously Bill's job satisfaction left something to be desired. His less-than-enthusiastic evaluation of his work begs the question of why did he feel that way about his job and why didn't he do something about it?

There are lots of people like Bill who feel trapped in a job or career and don't know what to do about it. As the saying goes, most people don't plan to fail, they just fail to plan. Because many people don't have a prudent earnings plan, their careers meander like running water taking the path of least resistance.

The path starts with enough scholastic success to open the doors to a broad range of career possibilities. The path then continues with less than ideal career choices among these possibilities, ones based upon practicality for geographical, relational, or financial reasons, or upon family tradition. It is practicality that reduces career options down to merely an expeditious acceptance of a job offer, instead of an intentional and proactive search for a career that is a tailored fit to one's natural personality gifts.

Because of the ease of most entry-level jobs and the diligence common to new careers, there may be some early career success that leads to a promotion. Then maybe there is more success and another promotion, and perhaps another repeat or two of this pattern. But what appears to be a career taking flight is one that is actually beginning to spin out of control. Each promotion leads to greater responsibility and greater pressure to perform.

Unfortunately, since the career was not originally chosen on the basis of one's strongest abilities, the person has limited talent, energy, and enthusiasm to meet the higher job demands. Eventually, the career stalls, and the worker is a victim of job-related burnout. The situation could have been avoided with a plan to earn money in a profession that was more suited to the person's s personality preferences. Ironically, the feelings of job burnout are often intensified by excessively spending money to alleviate the stress from earning it. This, then, creates a financial vise that squeezes from both the earning and spending ends with unbearable pressure.

We own a large, fourteen-year-old station wagon with a four cylinder engine. Its length of dependable service speaks to its character as a work horse. But we rarely go on long trips with it in extreme weather or hilly terrain because the strain on its engine is too great in those conditions. By taxing it for long periods under less than ideal conditions, we will eventually wear out its engine. Job burnout is much the same, in that it is usually not inspired by excess work but rather improper work that one is poorly suited for. Planning a career around one's natural gifts, talents and interests, instead of just looking for a job to work hard at, will reduce the likelihood of burnout.

Beware the Peter Principle

Another well-known career phenomenon is the Peter Principle, which states that all employees will rise in an organization until they reach their level of incompetence. The Peter Principle is the product of a well-intended but ill-conceived reward system found in many professions, especially large, hierarchical organizations. Like job-related burnout, I believe that the Peter Principle can be linked to personality type.

In the book *Type Talk*, authors Otto Kroeger and Janet M. Theusen stated that there is a direct link between job-level skills and personality type.[8] Career counselors generally use three categories to sort jobs into, those oriented around: data, including data entry, accounting, and inventory control; people, notably sales, teaching, and supervising; and things, such as the mechanical projects worked on by craftsmen and machine operators. The skills required at different levels of expertise in each category make different demands on one's personality type.

Entry level jobs in each category can be performed acceptably by nearly all types. In fact, type will probably have little to do with performance, although it may affect job satisfaction. For example, while the entering, copying, and basic computing of data may appeal to sensing types, these tasks are not too demanding for any personality type. Likewise, extraverts and

176

feelers may enjoy working in customer service, but no personality type should probably find this overwhelming.

However, at increasingly higher levels of complexity in all three career categories, types that manage complexity well—intuitives and perceivers—will tend to be more successful. Coordinating and synthesizing (data), mentoring or negotiating (people), and organizing materials or creating operating procedures (things), are all examples of jobs that require vision, creativity, and perceptivity. While these are skills that can be developed by all types, they are the natural talents of those with personality preferences for intuition and perception.

Unfortunately, it is precisely the intuitives and perceivers that are most likely to become frustrated by the relatively simplistic work at the lower levels of their career fields, reducing their chances of developing the experience or having the success necessary to rise to the top levels. This, then, increases the possibility that those who do climb up the career ladder are not the ones best suited for the higher level jobs, creating the Peter Principle, whereby people rise to their level of incompetence.

First noted by Professor Laurence Peter, the Peter Principle is often found in large organizations that have separate technical and management career paths. A well-deserved but potentially ill-fated reward for technical excellence in a specific job is a promotion into management. While the first management assignment probably still deals with many technical aspects, successively higher management posts will move further away from the day-to-day technical skills that were originally so valued, and more into broader issues of finance, research, and development, long-range planning, human resource development, facility management, strategic planning, risk management. These are all "big picture" issues that have to be seen in a "bottom line" perspective, a complex level of thinking that all types will not have equal facility with. That reality, however, is not discovered until the level of Peter Principle takes hold and the once productive employee reaches his personal level of incompetence.

Remember, the aim in career choices, just as in other aspects of life, is to find yourself in environments befitting your personality type preferences. The better the fit, the greater the enjoyment, the greater the productivity and the less the stress. With good planning based upon good self-awareness that personality type provides, you don't have to burn out, rise to your level of incompetence, or just always look forward to the weekend. You can have an energizing, satisfying *en theos* career in which you thrive.

CHAPTER ELEVEN

Modifying Your Money Style

> The wealth of a man is the number of things which he loves and blesses, which he is loved and blessed by.
>
> *—Thomas Carlyle*

It should be clear that discovering your money personality is both interesting and insightful. But is it financially profitable? The challenge now is to apply what you've learned about yourself in ways that are meaningful and productive. Knowledge only becomes power when it results in a life that's changed for the better. That's really what profit is—leaving a better person than when you started.

Successful money management requires three things. First, you must understand the technical aspects of how money works so that you know what it can be expected to do for you. This is the subject of the vast majority of books, magazines, and other educational material. It is my contention that the benefits of this knowledge is greatly overrated because, for the most part, the technical aspects of money are not that complicated.

Second, you must understand the relational aspects of money so that you know what people can be expected to do for you. Learning how to influence others to get what you want has become an expected and accepted part of our culture. While the relational aspects of money cannot be denied and should not be minimized, when this type of knowledge becomes self-centered manipulation rather than mutually beneficial co-operation, its benefits also become greatly overrated.

Third, you must understand the individual personality aspects of money so that you know what money has the potential for doing to you, positively or negatively. The benefits of this knowledge cannot be understated. It is my contention that the awareness of your money personality is the most critical of the requirements for successful money management.

However, while becoming aware of your money style is critical, it is only the first step to mastering your money. We must learn how to use these new insights about ourselves. This will mean doing more than merely identifying our influences, strengths, and weaknesses, as vital as that is. It will mean consciously using our strengths (which typically we take for granted) to achieve our desires. It will mean deciding not to be limited by the influences of our pasts. Whether guilt, envy, embarrassment, apathy, or fear, our emotional walls must come down if we are to master our money or we will continue to be held hostage by the financial fallacies living inside the walls.

Mastering your money personality begins with knowing and affirming who you are with regard to money. You must accept and approve who you are. You should appreciate your interests, the things you like to do; your values, what you are willing to do to get what you want; and your skills, your natural talents. Affirming yourself is a major factor in healthy self-esteem, which contributes to positive, successful behavior.

Affirming who you are will allow you to determine for yourself what will give you the greatest contentment. Recognize what your life currently is; that will prepare you for the path of personal fulfillment by realizing the potential of what life can be. The biggest factor in what life is at the present is you and your personality. Your personality is your greatest asset and greatest energy resource.

As cited in chapter 1, fewer Americans are "very happy" today than fifty years ago, despite spending twice as much money as then. Money cannot buy happiness if it is not used according to who we are. You will learn to enjoy your money only when you spend it to satisfy your real nature within your core personality.

Most of us need a new approach to personal money management, one that has the creature comforts of this century along with the emotional satisfaction that existed fifty years ago. These need not be mutually exclusive aims if we are willing to change our present money attitudes and actions to financial behaviors that are consistent with our money personalities.

THREE KEY STEPS TO CHANGE

Discovering your money personality is the vital prerequisite to producing a life-changing approach to your personal finances. The ultimate change will come with the completion of three steps. The first step is taking responsibility for your financial behaviors, past, present, and future. They are yours regardless of their source and if you don't like them, only you can decide to change them. The second step is reprogramming your attitude toward money. This will begin with redefining success in terms of contentment rather than financial accomplishment. The third step is developing a plan of attainable goals based upon a new definition of what it means to be a financial success. This will be achieved by learning how to spend money wisely.

Step 1: Take responsibility

According to personality type experts Otto Kroeger and Janet Theusen, life tends to support our preferences. Regardless of our type of money personality, we will tend to find that the day's financial events seem to take place according to our personality preferences. We should not be surprised at finding ourselves doing things that make us comfortable and avoiding activities or situations that make us uncomfortable. And in the face of uncertainty, we will trust our natural instincts.

Therefore, if you are a protector, you will feel good about any day that had financial activity, including thoughts, that brought structure and order to your life, and made you feel responsible about your financial stewardship. On the other hand, if you are a planner, you will feel good at the end of a day that found you preparing for your financial future or having demonstrated your expertise. Thinkers will feel good about finding a universal rule to apply to a tough financial decision, while feelers will be just as satisfied by finding a viable way to be financially supportive to someone in need.

Taking responsibility means owning your own behavior and its results regardless of outcomes and amount of outside influences. Keep this truth in mind: Your money personality may be highly predictive of your financial behavior before the fact, and may accurately account for your behavior after the fact, but *your money personality does not determine your behavior!* You should not blame poor financial actions on any part of your money personality because you have the freedom to make decisions and use appropriate action in every situation. While you will tend to go with your strengths, using a weakness may be the best response.

For example, it is a cop-out for a perceiver to say, "Hey, I can't stick to a budget. I need freedom and spontaneity, so how could anyone expect me to have the discipline for a budget?" On the other hand, a judger cannot use his budget as an excuse for passing up an unplanned opportunity. Likewise, a sensing type should not say, "Well, I haven't really planned for my retirement—I don't have any IRAs and I spent my built-up profit-sharing when I left Acme. But what do you expect? I focus on the now; that's what sensors are all about." The sensor's orientation to the immediate is no excuse for not preparing adequately for the future.

You are a unique individual with likes, dislikes, goals, and skills unlike anyone else. No one has the potential to know you as well as you do. Certainly, no one is going to care about your money as much as you do. Being responsible simply means being accountable as the primary cause for a particular outcome. Since it's you, your money, and your happiness that is at stake, it only makes sense (and cents!) to put that accountability into the hands of the person most qualified and most interested person in terms of achieving specific results— you!

Step 2: Changing your money attitude

Imagine having everything you ever wanted. Anything and everything your eyes desired was yours! Having it all and enjoying it all are both the same—a fantasy.

The richest man ever, King Solomon, did have it all. "Anything I wanted, I took," he said. "I did not restrain myself from any joy." Did his disregard for self-restraint actually bring him joy? What was the result of the unrestrained spending of his prodigious wealth? "But as I looked at everything I had worked so hard to accomplish, it was all so meaningless. It was like chasing the wind. There was nothing really worthwhile anywhere."[1]

Meaningless—all his accumulation seemed meaningless. Though each of us may define "significance" differently, the fact is we want our efforts to matter. Nothing galls us more than wasted effort, time, or resources. For proof, consider all the expressions we have created that deal with futility:

- "like talking to a brick wall"
- "a wild goose chase"
- "like a dog chasing its own tail"
- "Haste makes waste."
- "What a waste of [time, money, effort]."
- "All dressed up with nowhere to go."

Because we measure success by getting rather than by doing, our culture has indoctrinated us into thinking that having more is better than having less. As film writer Woody Allen said, "Money is better than poverty, if only for financial reasons."[2] Moreover, having money and possessions has become associated in modern society with having significance. Our culture pays attention to those who have wealth, the Bill Gateses, Donald Trumps, and Oprah Winfreys of society. Unfortunately, Solomon's life, which arguably represents the greatest level of human achievement ever, belies the truth that wealth means significance.

If, as Solomon said, having everything doesn't matter, then what does? Since it's obvious that money does matter, how do we give it meaning? What do we have to do to eliminate futility, frustration, and stress from our relationship with money? What do we really have to do to make money buy happiness?

Much of this book has been devoted to the premise that using money according to the preferences of your inborn personality will bring great satisfaction. But this is just the process, not the product; it's the road map, not the destination. The second step toward a truly wealthy financial life is to reprogram our money attitude. We must have a new attitude: *Financial success means being content with less, not seeking more.*

What does it mean to be content? According to *Webster's Ninth New Collegiate Dictionary,* the adjective *contented* means manifesting (making evident to the senses, especially the eye) satisfaction with one's possessions or status or situation. The verb *content* means to "to limit (oneself) in requirements, desires or actions."

In other words, true financial success can be achieved by attaining satisfaction with your money that others can see. This satisfied state will be accomplished by intentionally having less rather than more. And what ultimately will make this state so satisfactory is limiting yourself to that which matters most to you.

Achieving contentment with money does not require great skill. It's actually surprisingly easy. You can reach it by applying three financial contentment tips.

Financial Contentment Tip #1: Recognize that money is not recyclable.

A dollar, once it's spent, can never be spent again. That makes every spending decision a single, permanent, irreversible decision. In other words, money cannot be recycled. If you want to spend more money, you will need additional dollars.

Not only is money not recyclable, it cannot be in two places at once. In other words, a dollar spent on one thing precludes that dollar from being spent on something else. Because money cannot be in two places at once, each time you say "yes" to one purchase, you are saying "no" to all the other possible purchases that could have been made with that amount of money. Fifty dollars spent on groceries is fifty dollars that cannot be spent on clothes. To buy fifty dollars worth of clothes, you'll need an additional fifty dollars.

Financial Contentment Tip #2: Make a distinction between needs, wants, and desires.

Financial planners estimate that the typical American spends about 30 percent of their money unnecessarily. Given that money is nonrecyclable, this is especially worrisome. The reason for this is that most people don't make distinctions between needs, wants, and desires.

- Needs are the basic necessities of life: food, shelter, clothing, transportation, and health care. Spending decisions in the area of needs should almost always be "yes."

- Wants are needs of higher quality. This is where lifestyle decisions come into play. Where needs provide life's basic necessities at a minimally adequate level, wants upgrade your lifestyle for greater pleasure, comfort, and convenience. Choosing between a larger or smaller home, a luxury large or economy car, and filet mignon or ground beef all represent decisions between needs and wants. Clothing is a need, an extensive wardrobe is a want. Spending decisions in the area of wants should be "yes" or "no" depending on their affordability, and to some degree, how your money personality drives a particular lifestyle decision.

- Desires are everything else. This means that you neither need or even want a large screen television, a boat, a designer wardrobe, or new furniture every three years. While these and many other things certainly are enjoyable to own, none of these items are basic to increased comfort and convenience. Therefore, under no circumstances is a desire a need or a want. For reasons explained in Financial Contentment Tip #3 (page 186), most of your decisions in the area of desires should be "no."

Where most people end up in financial difficulty is by overspending because of their failure to make these distinctions. Our wants and desires are, in large part, determined by peer group and societal norms, and the pressure to conform is tremendous. That's why we think we "need" the things we decide to buy. Good yes and no spending decisions require discernment as to the proper classification of a prospective purchase.

Financial Contentment Tip #3. Orient your life around the fulfillment of the material things that matter most.

At seminars, I like to go around the room and ask people to name their one or two favorite ways to spend money. Rarely does anyone not have an immediate answer. "Clothes!" "Tools!" "Gardening" "Home electronics!" "CD's!" "Cars!" "Golfing!" "Going out to dinner!" One gentleman even said his favorite thing was gourmet pork and beans! The point is that we all have wired into our behavior passions for certain material possessions. Not only are they an expression to others of who we are, but without these things we would lose an important part of our capacity to enjoy life.

Your goal in personal money management is to *orient your life around the fulfillment of the material things that matter most.*

I call this the Golden Rule of personal finance. No matter what else you do as part of the process, and no matter how your life experience or inborn personality affects the process, the penultimate goal of money is to be content with what you have and that will happen when you orient your life around the fulfillment of the material things that matter most. Having everything—even if were possible—doesn't matter. What matters is that you fulfill your own unique passions that give you the greatest satisfaction.

From these three tips for financial contentment, it should be clear that many of us need to know what we want from life. That's why an understanding of your personality is so important, because we come into the world preprogrammed with core values and interests. However, as you mature, the culture infuses its values and standards for success into you. Unfortunately, the world won't give you much help in achieving success on its terms. That's why taking responsibility for your own financial success is so important.

It bears repeating that money is just a tool, one that allows us to live our lives in personally fulfilling ways. Just as it is futile for a craftsman to accumulate tools but never make anything satisfying, it likewise makes no sense to accumulate money and not have a fulfilling life. Therefore, simply amassing money and possessions is not a meaningful goal.

True financial success is having enough money to be content and most people are surprised at how little money that takes. It's not how much money you have, but how you use it that counts, and it is my conviction that if you have any money, you probably have enough to be content.

Step 3. How to Make Wise Money Decisions

Learning to make wise money decisions is one skill that will help you tremendously in your pursuit of financial contentment. I like to define *wisdom* as *the best means to the best ends.* The good news for those who have been frustrated by their lack of skill in money matters is that skill is not necessary for success. King Solomon used great means but failed to achieve his desired ends. Robin Hood had great ends (giving to the poor) but used questionable means (stealing from the rich) to achieve them. There can be little doubt that both men had great skill in money matters, yet their efforts were futile and illegitimate.

Almost everything that you do with money is an act of perception (finding things out), or an act of judgment (deciding). To be successful at managing money, or anything else, requires perceiving and then judging, in that order. Recall that there are two methods of perception, or taking in information, either through sensing or through intuition. The sensing function likes to take in information that is real and tangible, "right here, right now," by using the senses of sight, smell, touch, taste, and hearing to gather specific, detailed information. The intuitive function likes to take in information by seeing the big picture and making connections to other information that's related to the present facts.

Everybody has a preference for one or the other, and through constant use will usually become more proficient at using their preference than their nonpreference. Sensing types will become expert at noticing things, recalling facts observed from past experience, then focusing their attention on the present. Intuitives will be more expert at seeing possibilities, connections, and relationships, and then focusing their attention on the future.

Once you have used a perceptive function to find things out, you will employ a judgment function to make a decision based upon the information you gathered. Recall that there are two ways of deciding, either using thinking or feeling. Thinking judgments are based upon your impersonal, logical "true and false" assessment of the information, weighing the consequences of each course of action. Feeling judgments are based upon what is important to you and any other people involved.

Again, everybody has a preference for one or the other and will tend to become more proficient at their preference than their nonpreference. Thinkers will become adept at finding the principles necessary to make a decision while feelers will naturally focus on the principals—the people—and make their decision accordingly. Doing this will lead you on the road to wise money decisions.

Each of the four mental functions—sensing and intuition, thinking and feeling—are our natural gifts given to us at birth to manage the present and forge the future, to find truth and relate interpersonally to others.

USING OUR DOMINANT FUNCTION
IN MAKING WISE DECISIONS

We must appropriately utilize all four mental functions, while relying on our dominant preference in each function. Becoming expert in using our dominant function is the first step to getting on the pathway of financial success. The kind of perception (sensing or intuition) or judgment (thinking or feeling) most natural to us points us in the direction of our greatest potential and most likely road to contentment. Then we need to develop our auxiliary processes to give our personalities good balance. An inadequate auxiliary process is easy to spot. For example, perceiving without adequate judgment is tolerant of too much. Judging without adequate perceiving is very narrow-minded.

Of course, we should not rely solely on our favored functions to the exclusion of the others. Wise decisions in the management of our finances requires the use of all four functions, therefore, we must make good use of our least favored processes when it is appropriate to do so.

For example, with a personality type of ENTP, I prefer to make decisions using intuition (N) and thinking (T). My first inclination is to use intuition to gather information that is conceptual, global, and future oriented in nature, and then use thinking to decide after an impersonal analysis of the data. On the other hand, I do not prefer to make decisions using sensing and feeling. This means that I tend not to gather information that is specific, detailed, and oriented to the present, nor make decisions that prioritizes people over principles.

However, depending upon a given situation, my less preferred functions may be the best to use to make a decision. If I consistently neglect to use my nonpreferred functions, my life will be out of balance. My nonpreferred functions will be immature, unable to provide adequate insight when needed and therefore, produce unreliable results.

Using Perception

When it comes to your dominant perception, recognize that at various times *each* way of gathering information is needed. *Sensing* is needed to gather information that is useful for managing the practical, day-to-day matters of one's finances, like keeping records, tracking expenses, and employing myriad ways to save money. On the other hand, *intuition* is more useful to gather information relevant to one's future, for instance, retirement planning; developing broad financial plans that integrate tax, estate, insurance, and investment plans; or developing strategic plans like career planning or debt reduction.

The intuitive's error is too much focus on the future to the exclusion of present realities and current limitations. The failure to acknowledge or attend to present conditions can render their glorious possibilities impossible. Without input from the sensing function, intuitives will change for the sake of change and inattentively ignore or discard what is working in the present.

By contrast, the sensing type's error is to assume that what exists at the present, is all that ever can be. They may restrict the possibilities of the future with their boundaries of past experience of presently perceived limitations. Without input from the intuition function, sensing types may be unwilling or unable to change their current circumstances for the better or react to information with which they have no experience.

Each function needs the other to ensure all the relevant data is available to begin the decision-making process.

Using Judgment

When it comes to your dominant judgment, recognize that at various times *each* element, thinking and feeling, is needed in different situations. Either thinking or feeling can be the best kind of judgment in a certain situation.

Consider how thinkers and feelers add to a financial decision. Thinkers will focus on the data aspects of a decision: buying at the right price, at the right place, at the right time, for the right reasons, and spending the right amount given what's affordable. They will decide based on logic and efficiency. By contrast, feelers are skilled at seeing the impact on others that a financial decision will have. The impact of a decision on one's financial condition is not nearly as important as what personal values are upheld by the decision. Deciding in terms of their own priorities and others' needs and wants is the feeler's most important business. They find their satisfaction in doing the right thing given the people involved.

Just like we need to access information through both sensing and intuition, we also need to be able to evaluate information by both thinking and feeling.

Using *All* the Functions

Wise decisions can be arrived at by allowing each function to play its unique role at the right time as follows:

- *Sensing* to gather specific facts and realities. To activate your sensing process, ask yourself how the situation would look to an observant, impartial bystander.

- *Intuition* to see patterns, associations, connections, and possibilities. To activate your intuition, try to avoid the "not invented here" syndrome by not automatically assuming that what you have been doing is right.

- *Thinking* to ask yourself, "Is this right or wrong?" To activate your thinking judgment, look to find a universal rule that can be consistently applied to a decision under consideration.

- *Feeling* to ask yourself, "How do I feel about this?" To activate your feeling judgment, remember that feelings and emotions you or others may experience are relevant facts to be considered in the decision-making process.

The final result will be a wise decision, one that uses the best means to arrive at the best ends, because there has been an appropriate consideration of the facts, possibilities, consequences, and human values.

The ability to make wise decisions is not natural but can be acquired by practice. It will require you to consciously put into use the strengths of other personality types that are, in fact, your weaknesses. Keep in mind that your weaknesses would be associated with the mental processes (sensing, intuition, thinking, feeling) that are not part of your four-letter MBTI description. The least used function according to your personality type is called the *inferior function;* the function opposite the secondary (or auxiliary) function is called the *tertiary function.*

The skills listed by type in the table below are deficient because they have rarely been put into practice. For most of your life these processes have been blind spots, and your behavior has been affected by their neglect.

Table 13

TERTIARY AND INFERIOR
FUNCTIONS OF EACH TYPE

In this table, the dominant process is shown in boldface

ISTJ Feeling Intuition	**ISFJ** Thinking Intuition	**INFJ** Thinking Sensing	**INTJ** Feeling Sensing
ISTP Intuition Feeling	**ISFP** Intuition Thinking	**INFP** Sensing Thinking	**INTP** Sensing Feeling
ESTP Feeling Intuition	**ESFP** Thinking Intuition	**ENFP** Thinking Sensing	**ENTP** Feeling Sensing
ESTJ Intuition Feeling	**ESFJ** Intuition Thinking	**ENFJ** Sensing Thinking	**ENTJ** Sensing Feeling

According to Isabel Briggs Myers, the two best ways to develop your deficient tertiary and inferior processes is to:

- "let them play" in recreational outlets. Sensors should challenge their intuition with reading or "mind games" like crossword puzzles. Intuitives should dabble in sensory activities like exercise or crafts.

- enlist the weaker functions in support of a goal that appeals to your dominant process; in other words, use a weakness to support your strengths. For instance, a sensing-feeler who wants to take a family vacation might use intuition to develop a spending plan to save the money and then make spending decisions according to the monthly budget to achieve the future goal.

FINDING WEALTH

Over sixty-thousand people earn more than a million dollars per year but how many are truly wealthy?

Wealth is not a state of assets but a state of mind! Because true wealth is a state of mind, it will not be measured by financial assets but by:

- the degree that you feel in control of your money and your emotions about money; and

- the amount of emotional satisfaction rather than amount of assets accumulation that you derive from earning, spending, and saving money.

True wealth comes from recognizing and appreciating the rich fabric of your personality. Your personality is a gift that allows you to enjoy life in ways that are unique to you. Understanding the role that money plays in our lives can unlock the door to new fields of self-awareness that direct us to new ways of relating to money. Discovering your money personality can expose hidden weaknesses and reveal previously unacknowledged strengths. A greater understanding of who you are may give you the confidence to explore your personal finances at a much deeper level than you ever dared to before.

The challenge you face is whether you use this knowledge profitably, making yourself better through the process of managing your money. As Henry Ford said, "The highest use of capital is not to make more money, but to make money do more for the betterment of life."

Real Wealth: An Eternal Perspective

> A man's treatment of money is the most deci-
> sive test of his character—how he makes it and
> how he spends it.
>
> —*C. Wright Mills*

For most Americans, the desire for financial freedom through financial wealth is an illusory and quixotic quest. Alexis de Toqueville wrote that in America, people "can never attain as much as they desire. It perpetually retires from before them, yet without hiding itself from their sight, and in retiring draws them on. At every moment they think they are about to grasp it; it escapes at every moment from their hold."[1]

True wealth is a holistic sense of overall well-being that no amount of money alone can buy. Money is just a tool that one can use to become wealthy by:

- accepting that money is not an end but a means to an end. That end will be defined in large part by your "utiles," your personal psychological assessment of how useful things or activities are to you;

- having a realistic view of what money can be expected to accomplish for you by rejecting financial fallacies that have been blocking your path to true wealth; and

- managing your money personality: understanding the actions and attitudes that determine your financial behavior; then being willing to modify those aspects of your financial behavior that have prevented you from achieving true wealth.

This holistic sense of well-being, which money cannot buy, gets to the deeper issues of our lives—our personal values. With that in mind, I cannot ignore a source of great insight on money and life, the Holy Scriptures.

I believe that there are universal rules about everything, standards of thinking and conduct designed to govern our lives for our highest well-being. While the infinite differences in our money personalities suggest infinite paths to wealth, there still has to be a universal standard of truth that all can compare their attitudes and actions against. Such rules would reflect the ultimate in wisdom—the best possible means to the best possible ends for all.

I have mentioned God and quoted from the Bible at several points in this book. The Bible, the best-selling book in history, remains the source of principles and laws for this country. A recent survey reported in the *Washington Post* found that nearly seven out of ten Americans believe in a "perfect, all powerful creator" they call God.[2] I trust my mentioning God and the Bible does not surprise many readers.

Like so many others, I believe that the God of the Bible is the perfect, all powerful creator. In an incredible act of love and desire to relate personally to the people He created, He told us all about Himself in the Bible. Because He is perfect in character and nature, He must be the source of all that is true. Therefore, there are universal rules and principles that govern every aspect of life, including money. These principles cut across culture, generations, stages of life, and personality type.

THE BIBLE: A GUIDEBOOK ON MONEY

While most people have had some exposure to the Bible, few know how much of its teachings focus on money. Many people are surprised to learn the Bible has financial principles. In fact, one survey found that only 51 percent of people believed that the Bible contained any guidance in the area of money.

The subject of money is actually one of the Bible's dominant themes. Sixteen of Jesus Christ's parables refer to money; more is said in the New Testament about money than about heaven and hell combined; fives times more is said about money than prayer; and while there are 500 verses on both prayer and faith, there are nearly 2,500 verses dealing with money and possessions.

As one might expect, some of the Bible's teachings on money are philosophical: "For the love of money is a root of all kinds of evil." As one might also expect, some teachings are moral in nature: "The wicked borrow and do not repay."[3] The familiar words, "It is more blessed to give than receive,"[4] were Jesus' own summary on the subject of charity. Naturally, this is not the kind of advice that one typically finds in personal finance books. Yet, much of what are considered basic tenets of money management actually find their source in the Bible!

For example, consider these Scriptures on how to handle our money:

- On debt: "Just as the rich rule the poor, so the borrower is servant to the lender" (Proverbs 22:7).
- On saving: "The wise have wealth and luxury, but fools spend whatever they get" (Proverbs 21:20).
- On investing for the future: "Take a lesson from the ants . . . they labor hard all summer, gathering food for the winter" (Proverbs 6:6, 8).
- On diversification: "Be sure to stay busy and plant a variety of crops, for you never know which will grow" (Ecclesiastes 11:6).
- On risk management: "The prudent see danger and take refuge, but the simple keep going and suffer for it" (Proverbs 27:12).
- On financial planning: "Be sure you know the condition of your flocks, give careful attention to your herds" (Proverbs 27:23) [5]

Why are these and other Biblical principles of money management so important? They are important because of one universal truth: God created people in His own image; God patterned them after Himself.[6]

A significant part of this image is our personality. Since this personality is God-given, it was designed to reflect His character and nature in our own behavior. Moreover, when we are behaving in ways consistent with our God-given personality, we are reaching our highest potential.

That's what makes answering the question of "What will I do with my money?" so critical. What we do with our money is determined in large part by our personalities, which have been completely predetermined by our Creator. Therefore, the more we know about who we are and what our Creator made us to do, the more likely it is that we will find answers to our money questions.

In that regard, I can think of one universal rule about money, one so well-known that it is called the Golden Rule: *Do unto others as you would have them do unto you.*[7] Our personalities characterize what we would like done "unto us." Awareness of personalities can guide us as to what we should "do unto others." Money is so pervasive in our lives that it gives us a greater opportunity to do unto others and have done unto us than probably anything else. Not only will using money according to our inborn personalities bring us the greatest satisfaction, it honors God, honors others, and honors the best of what lies within us.

The great theologian and hymn writer John Wesley said, "Get all you can without hurting your soul, your body, or your neighbor. Save all you can, cutting off every needless expense. Give all you can." That's what you should do with your money, no matter what type of personality you have.

Notes

Introduction: A New Approach to Money Management

1. National Opinion Center surveys reported by Richard Gene Niemi, John Mueller, and Tom W. Smith, *Trends in Public Opinion: A Compendium of Survey Data* (New York: Greenwood Press, 1989); cited in David G. Myers, "Society in the Balance: America's Social Recession and Renewal," (draft paper presented at Christianity Today Institute Global Stewardship Conference, Chicago, 14–16 March 1996), 10–11.

Chapter 1: The Value of Money

1. Warwick Webb, "Money Stress Blamed in 3 Deaths," *Fairfax Journal,* 5 August 1998, 1.

2. Illustration adapted from David T. Moore," Money Myths," *Because Money Matters,* audio tape series (Palm Desert, Calif.: Southwest Community Church, 1992).

3. Gary D. Kinnaman, *Mastering Your Money, Part 1: Beating the System: Strategies for the Helpless Consumer,* cassette tape (Mesa, Ariz.: Word of Grace Church, no date).

4. Richard Gene Niemi, John Mueller, and Tom Smith, *Trends in Public Opinion: A Compendium of Survey Data* (New York: Greenwood Press, 1989); personal correspondence with Tom Smith, *National Opinion Research Center;* and *Historical Statistics of the U.S. and Economic Indicators;* as cited in David G. Myers, "Society in the Balance: America's Social Recession and Renewal," 26 February 1996 (draft paper presented at Christianity Today Global Stewardship Conference, Chicago, 14–16 March 1996), 10.

5. *Historical Statistics of the U.S. and Economic Indicators;* as cited in David G. Myers, "Society in the Balance: America's Social Recession and Renewal," (draft paper presented at Christianity Today Global Stewardship Conference, Chicago, 14–16 March 1996), 2.

6. Olivia Mellan: *Money Harmony: Resolving Money Conflicts in Your Life and Relationships* (New York: Walker and Company, 1994), 17.

7. See Matthew 6:33. This is part of Jesus' famous Sermon on the Mount, which has much to say about how we use our money. See, for instance, Matthew 6:19–33.

Chapter 2: Your Money Memories

1. Linda Barbanel, *Money, Sex and Power* (New York: Macmillan Spectrum, 1996), 13.
2. Ibid., 13–15.
3. This attitude frequently is based upon a false understanding of the Bible passage 1 Timothy 6:10, which reads, "For the love of money is a root of all kinds of evil."

Chapter 3: Financial Fallacies

1. See Matthew 20:20–28, where Jesus said people should not desire to exert authority over other, but rather serve them.
2. Proverbs 22:3, NLT.
3. Rosalie Maggio, comp., *Money Talks: Quotations on Money and Investing* (Paramus, N. J.: Prentice Hall, 1998), 197.
4. The extent of Solomon's wealth is recorded in 1 Kings 10:14–25; the queen's response can be found in 1 Kings 10:1–8.
5. See Ecclesiastes 2:10–11; 5:10.
6. Proverbs 14:30. The tenth commandment is found in Exodus 20:17.
7. The Scriptures call both wealth and possessions and our ability to enjoy them "a gift of God"; see Ecclesiastes 5:19–20.
8. Proverbs 4:7; 17:16.
9. Ted Goodman, ed., *The Forbes Business Book of Quotations* (New York: Black Dog and Leventhal Publishers, 1997), 590.
10. Ibid., 587.
11. Proverbs 3:13–15, TLB.

Chapter 4: Money and Self-Esteem

1. *Dr. James Dobson's Focus on the Family Bulletin,* June 1989. Published by Tyndale of Carol Stream, Ill.
2. A few of the many New Testament verses that describe God's love for us are Romans 5:8; 1 John 4:16; and John 15:9, 13.
3. Matthew 6:24.
4. *All Consuming Passion,* 2nd ed. (Seattle: New Road Map Foundation, 1993), 6.
5. Bonnie J. Golden and Kay Lesh, *Building Self-Esteem: Strategies for Success in School and Beyond,* 2nd ed. (Upper Saddle River, N. J.: Gorsuch Scarisbrick Publishers, 1997), 58.
6. Marc Fisher, "Women Shop, Men Buy," *The Washington Post Magazine,* 22 August 1999, 19.
7. Golden and Lesh, *Building Self-Esteem,* 61.
8. Ibid., 60.

Chapter 5: You've Got Personality

1. The Myers-Briggs Type Indicator and MBTI are trademarks of Consulting Psychologist Press, Inc.

2. If you desire a more in-depth assessment and interpretation by taking the MBTI, you can write to Family Financial Concepts, Inc., 21264 Mirror Ridge Place, Sterling, VA 20164, or send E-mail to info@Goodstewardship.com.

3. Statements for the extravert/introvert dimension, as well as the sensor/intuitive, thinker/feeler, and judger/perceiver dimensions, are adapted from questions appearing in Paul D. Tieger and Barbara Barron-Tieger, *The Art of Speedreading People* (Boston: Little, Brown and Company, 1998), 13–17, 19–22, 24–34.

4. Paul D. Tieger and Barbara Barron-Tieger: *The Art of Speedreading People* (Boston: Little, Brown and Company, 1998), 18.

5. Ibid., 23.

6. To avoid confusion, the MBTI model uses *N* for intuition because *I* has already been used for introversion.

7. Tieger and Barron-Tieger: *The Art of Speedreading People,* 29.

8. Ibid., 34.

9. As quoted in Gordon Lawrence, *People Type and Tiger Stripes,* 3rd. ed. (Gainesville, Ga.: Center for Applications of Psychological Type, 1993), 17.

Chapter 6: What's Your Temperament?

1. David Keirsey: *Please Understand Me II,* (Del Mar, Calif.: Prometheus Nemesis, 1998), 26. Keirsey also noted temperament classifications by Plato (c. 340 B.C.), Aristotle (c. 325 B.C.), Galen (c. 190 B.C.), Adickes (1905), Spränger (1914), and Kretschmer (1920).

2. Jack Whelan, "American Soul," *Ions Noetic Sciences Review,* April–July 1999, 22–31.

3. Otto Kroeger and Janet M. Theusen, *Type Talk* (New York: Dell, 1988), 50.

4. Keirsey, *Please Understand Me II,* 26.

5. Kroeger and Theusen, *Type Talk,* 56.

6. The listing of well-known historical figures who fit the protector, as well as the listings for historical figures on the remaining temperaments come from this author and from Linda V. Berens, *Understanding Yourself and Others* (Huntington Beach, Calif.: Temperament Research Institute, Telos Publications, 1998), 25.

7. Kroeger and Theusen, *Type Talk,* 59.

8. Ibid., 53.

9. Ibid., 55.

10. Stephen R. Covey, *The Seven Habits of Highly Effective People* (New York: Simon and Schuster, 1989), 70.

Chapter 7: Your Financial Behavior

1. Susan A. Brock, *Using Type in Selling* (Palo Alto, Calif.: Consulting Psychologists Press, 1994), 14.

Chapter 8: Conquest or Conciliation: Money and Marriage

1. As quoted in Joe Dominguez and Vicki Robin, *Your Money or Your Life,* (New York: Penguin, 1992), xx.

2. Sherri Dalphonse, "Love and Money," *Washingtonian,* February 2000, 48; "Handling Money Problems," in Clayton E. Tucker-Ladd, *Psychological Self-Help* (Dublin, Ohio: Mental Health Net, 1999) at www.mentalhelp.net/psyhelp/chap10/chap10i.htm; Internet, accessed on 20 January 2000.

3. Trimark Investment Management, Inc., "Talking About Money," at Trimark website: www.trimark.ca/Trimark/Retail/InvestorEd; Internet, accessed on 20 January 2000.

4. Recall from chapter 5 that 65 percent of women have a preference for making judgments using a feeling process, and that 65 percent of men have a preference for making judgments using a thinking process.

5. Isabel Briggs Myers, *Gifts Differing* (Palo Alto, Calif.: Davies-Black, 1995), 124.

6. Jane Hardy Jones and Ruth G. Sherman, *Intimacy and Type* (Gainesville, Ga.: Center for the Application of Psychological Type, 1997), 17.

7. Empathic listening is a term used by Stephen R. Covey, *The 7 Habits of Highly Effective People* (New York: Simon and Schuster, 1989), 236–60. My thoughts on mature listening have been greatly influenced by Covey's Habit 5, "Seek first to understand, then to be understood."

8. Stephen R. Covey, *The 7 Habits of Highly Effective People* (New York: Simon and Schuster, 1989), 241.

Chapter 9: "Honey, Let's Talk Money!"

1. Steve Myers, *Influencing People Using Myers Briggs* (Wirral, England: Team Technology, 1995), 54.

2. Carl Jung hypothesized such difficulties years ago. Jane Hardy Jones and Ruth G. Sherman, *Intimacy and Type* (Gainesville, Ga.: Center for the Application of Psychological Type, 1997), 68.

Chapter 10: Suit Yourself to a Custom-Tailored Career

1. David T. Moore, "Money Myths," *Because Money Matters* audio tape series, (Palm Desert, Calif.: Southwest Community Church, 1992).

2. Ecclesiastes 5:20.

3. Paul D. Tieger and Barbara Barron-Tieger, *Do What You Are,* 2nd ed. (Boston: Little, Brown, 1995), 3.

4. Richard Bolles, *What Color Is My Parachute?* (Berkeley, Calif.: Ten Speed Press, 1996), 449.

5. Ecclesiastes 5:19.

6. Isabel Briggs Myers, *Gifts Differing* (Palo Alto, Calif.: Davies-Black, 1995), 149.

7. Earle C. Page, *Organizational Tendencies* (Gainesville: Center for Applications for Psychological Type, 1985); as cited in Sandra Krebs Hirsh and Jean M. Kummerow, *Introduction to Type in Organizations,* 2nd ed. (Palo Alto, Calif.: Consulting Psychologists Press, 1990), 12.

8. Otto Kroeger and Janet M. Theusen, *Type Talk* (New York: Dell, 1988), 192.

Chapter 11: Modifying Your Money Style

1. Ecclesiastes 2:10–11 NLT.

2. *Money Talks, Quotations on Money and Investing* compiled by Rosalie Maggio (Paramus: Prentice Hall Press, 1998), 11.

Epilogue: Real Wealth: An Eternal Perspective

1. Marc Fisher, "Naming Your Price—Many Americans Find That the Money They Desire Is Never Quite Enough," *Washington Post,* 30 June 1997, C1.
2. Bill Broadway, "Poll Finds America 'as Churched as Ever,'" *Washington Post,* 31 May 1997, B7.
3. 1 Timothy 6:10; Psalm 37:21.
4. Acts 20:35.
5. The first four verses are from the New Living Translation; the final two are from the New International Version.
6. See Genesis 1:27.
7. The so-called Golden Rule, announced by Jesus of Nazareth, is found in Matthew 7:12 and Luke 6:31.

APPENDIX ONE

The Sixteen Personality Types

These descriptions of the sixteen personality types should help you confirm your type, as intitially determined in chapter 5.

ISTJ	ISFJ	INFJ	INTJ
"Doing what should be done"	"A high sense of duty"	"An inspiration to others"	"Everything has room for improvement"
Organizer	Amiable	Reflective/	Theory based
Compulsive	Works behinds	introspective	Skeptical
Private	the scenes	Quietly caring	"My way"
Trustworthy	Ready to sacri-	Creative	High need for
Rules	fice	Linguistically	competency
Practical	Accountable	gifted	Sees world as
	Prefers "doing"	Psychic	chessboard
Most Responsible	*Most Loyal*	*Most Contemplative*	*Most Independent*

ISTP	ISFP	INFP	INTP
"Ready to try anything once"	"Sees much but shares little"	"Performing noble service to aid society"	"A Love of problem solving"
Very observant Cool and aloof Hands-on practicality Unpretentious Ready for what happens	Warm and sensitive Unassuming Short-range Planner Good team member In touch with self and nature	Strict personal values Seeks inner order/peace Creative Non-directive Reserved	Challenges other to think Absent-minded professor Competency needs Socially cautious
Most Pragmatic	*Most Artistic*	*Most Idealistic*	*Most Conceptual*

ESTP	ESFP	ENFP	ENTP
"The ultimate realist"	"You only go around once in life"	"Giving life an extra squeeze"	"One exciting challenge after another"
Unconventional approach Fun Gregarious Lives for here and now Good at problem solving	Sociable Spontaneous Loves surprises Cuts red tape Juggles multiple projects/events Quip master	People oriented Creative Seeks harmony Life of party More starts than finishes	Argues both sides of a point to learn Brinksmanship Tests the limits Enthusiastic New ideas
Most Spontaneous	*Most Generous*	*Most Optimistic*	*Most Inventive*

The Sixteen Personality Types

ESTJ	**ESFJ**	**ENFJ**	**ENTJ**
"Life's administrators"	"Host and hostesses of the world"	"Smooth talking persuader"	"Life's natural leaders"
Order and structure Sociable Opinionated Results driven Producer Traditional	Gracious Good interpersonal skills Thoughtful Appropriate Eager to please	Charismatic Compassionate Possibilities for people Ignores the unpleasant Idealistic	Visionary Gregarious Argumentative Systems planners Take charge Low tolerance for incompetency
Most Hard Charging	*Most Harmonizing*	*Most Persuasive*	*Most Commanding*

SOURCE: "The TypeWatching ToolKit"; Otto Kroeger Associates (Telephone: 703-591-6284.) Version 1.2 software, copyright 1998, Otto Kroeger Associates, Fairfax, VA. Used by permission.

What Are
Your Preferences?

According to your personality type, you will have a distinct source of energy and a distinct way of gathering information (finding things out), making decisions, and orienting your life. Within each type, one of four preferences dominate. The following charts will help you verify which of each of the four preferences dominate. This exercise will help you affirm your preferences in chapter 5.

Do you prefer to focus your energy each day around people or in private, introspective contemplation? Determine which list best describes the way you receive energy and inspiration (via people or ideas and reflection); then circle either *extraversion* or *introversion.*

Extraversion	Introversion
interaction	concentration
external	internal
breadth	depth
extensive	intensive
free disclosure	cautious disclosure
expressive	reserved
initiating	responding
think out loud	quiet reflection

Do you prefer to find things out by sensing or intuition? Determine which list best describes the way you gather information; then circle either *sensing* or *intuition.*

Sensing	Intuition
facts	possibilities
details	overview
present	future
enjoyment	anticipation
realistic	conceptual
actual	theoretical
specific	general
literal	figurative
practical	innovative

Do you prefer to decide by thinking or feeling? Determine which list best describes the way you make decisions; then circle either *thinking* or *feeling.*

Thinking	Feeling
analytically	sympathetically
objectively	subjectively
critically	appreciatively
as an onlooker	as a participant
on principles	on principals
clarity	harmony
nonpersonal	personal
justice	mercy
firm minded	fair hearted

Do you perfer to organize your life by judging or perceiving? Determine which list best describes the way you orient your life; then circle either *judging* or *perceiving.*

Judging	Perceiving
resolved	pending
control	adapt
closure	openness
planned	tentative

scheduled	spontaneous
decisive	impulsive
time driven	event driven
opinions	options
fixed	flexible

Based on my response, my preferences are:

Extravert or Introvert   **Sensor or Intuitive**

Thinker or Feeler   **Judger or Perceiver**

"If only I had a little more money!"

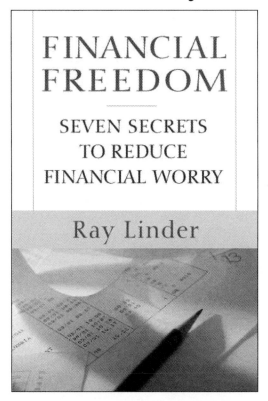

Financial Freedom
Seven Secrets to Reduce Financial Worry

In a society where being financially well-off is everything, take a look at what God says about money and our use of it. See how changing your attitude about what you have can really set you free. Gain a new perspective on your finances and reduce financial worry with these seven helpful truths.

Quality Paperback 0-8024-8196-5

If you are interested in information
about other books written from a
biblical perspective, please write
to the following address:

Northfield Publishing
215 West Locust Street
Chicago, IL 60610